Voices in American Education:

CONVERSATIONS with

Patricia Biehl ● Derek Bok ● Daniel Callahan
Robert Coles ● Edwin Dorn
Georgie Anne Geyer ● Henry Giroux
Ralph Ketcham ● Christopher Lasch
Elizabeth Minnich ● Frank Newman
Robert Payton ● Douglas Sloan
Manfred Stanley

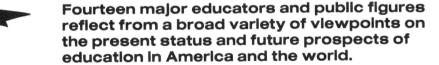

**Fourteen major educators and public figures
reflect from a broad variety of viewpoints on
the present status and future prospects of
education in America and the world.**

For

Loyd Easton

Friend and Mentor Over Many Years

VOICES IN AMERICAN EDUCATION
By Bernard Murchland
Published by Prakken Publications, Inc.
  Post Office Box 8623
  Ann Arbor, Michigan 48107
ISBN 0-911168-77-X
Library of Congress Catalog Card Number 89-062017

Contents

Epigraph

Let us understand then, that is should be our aim in learning, not merely to know the one thing which is to be our principal occupations, as well as it can be known, but to do this and also to know something about the great subjects of human interest . . . remembering that our object should be to obtain a true view of nature and life in their broad outline.

—John Stuart Mill

Preface

A Curious Time

IT is a curious time in American education. The cry for reform is heard everywhere in the land, but very few reforms take place. Between the rhetoric and the reality, our lack of resolution falls like a bundle board. This is not to say that no reforms have taken place. Some have. But they are not adequate to offset the general deterioration of standards which has by now become systemic. It is clearer to us than it has ever been that the public school system in America has been a failure. The grand design for education in a democratic society as conceived by John Dewey and others has to be rethought. "The condition of urban education is a national disgrace," is the way Ernest Boyer, president of the Carnegie Foundation for the Advancement of Teaching, puts it. Albert Shanker, president of the American Federation of Teachers, reports on a survey which showed that only 4.9 percent of high school graduates could figure out which train to take to get from Philadelphia to Washington. That sounds like a joke, but we know it isn't. Shanker says that schools are organized in ways that prevent most students from learning.

I have a colleague who assumes that by the time students reach college their minds are already ruined. By that he means that they have neither the desire nor the ability to think. My colleague is a philosopher and has rather high demands, so he is prone to exaggerate. Still, one sees his point. As a result of my own informal exit polling of graduating college seniors over a number of years, I know that the vast majority of them lack essential marks of an educated person. They do not have a love of learning; they are largely ignorant of our rich cultural heritages; they have virtually no civic commitment and no sense whatsoever of the sacred—that subtle blend of sensuality and spirituality which constitutes one of the finest flowers of the liberal arts tradition. In other words, they are pretty ignorant. But we must not yield too easily to the temptation of blaming the victims. Students are shrewd consumers, and they reflect quite faithfully the general values of their society. As my friend Ben Barber wrote in an OpEd piece in *The New York Times*: "There is ample evidence to suggest that the kids are smart, not stupid—smarter than we give them credit for. They are society-smart rather than school-smart. They are adept readers—but not of books. What they read so acutely are the social signals that emanate from the world in which they have to make their living. Their teachers in this world—the nation's true pedagogues—are television, advertising, movies, politics, and the celebrity domains they define. What our 17-year-olds know is exactly what our 47-year-olds know and, by their example, teach them."

We ought to note, too, that the American system of education actually operates on the principle of triage. At the bottom, there is great waste, but at the top our achievements can be quite remarkable. That is why the best schools are graduate schools. But this makes for a very lopsided system and skews educational values in lamentable ways. The basic problem, as I see it, is that we have not been able to connect learning with citizenship in any effective manner, and in a democracy that is a disaster. Many of my interlocutors see the problem in much the same way, which is why there is almost as much talk about citizenship as there is about education. We can't talk about the one without talking about the other. We can't solve the problems of the one without solving the problems of the other.

I am very grateful to those who took the time to be interviewed for this book. One cannot be ultimately despairing of an educational system that produced such voices! They sustain my hope. I am also grateful to the Kettering Foundation for support over the years. The Kettering Foundation, under the leadership of David Mathews, is doing more than any other body in the country to reconnect the promises of democracy with the imperatives of liberal learning. I also want to thank my friend and colleague, Bob Flanagan, who is a fertile source of metaphors.

Most of these interviews were published in some form or other in

The Kettering Review, The Antaeus Report, Reflections on America, The Civic Arts Review, and *Citizenship Education News*. My own essay was first published in *Commonweal* magazine. All are reprinted here with permission.

—Bernard Murchland

An Interview with
PATRICIA BIEHL on

A Walk Through the
Valley of Death

THE evidence mounts that the onus of educational reform lies at the
secondary level. And therein rests a paradox. For no group is less
empowered to undertake educational reform than high school
teachers. The dimensions of the problem are well expressed in a letter
to Ann Landers. The writer pointed out that in the 1940s and 1950s
teachers had to contend with students not getting homework done on
time and routine disciplinary problems; in the 1980s, the problems
are on the order of drugs, pregnancy, and assault. As a consequence,
high school teachers are leaving the profession in record numbers.

For the sake of simplicity, we can divide recent educational reform
efforts in America into three phases. The first was in response to the
launching of Sputnik into space in 1957. The second were the reforms
undertaken in the aftermath of the student revolts in the late 1960s.
And the third, which in a real sense constitutes evidence that the first
two efforts failed or at least were inadequate, was marked by the
publication of *A Nation at Risk* on April 27, 1983. That report
resonated throughout the land and made famous the expression "a
rising tide of mediocrity." Five years later, Secretary of Education
William Bennett commemorated that occasion with a report of his
own entitled *American Education: Making it Work*. He noted the
progress that had been made since 1983. But he was at pains to point
out that although schools had improved, they had not improved

enough. Bennett's report, as did its predecessor, emphasized the importance of recruiting, training, and rewarding good teachers. Bennett wrote, "We cannot expect our schools to improve, nor our children to achieve, so long as we adhere to a hiring and promotion system that rewards longevity over performance; that puts more stock in paper credentials than in knowledge, energy, and enthusiasm; and that pretends good teachers and good principals are to be found only among graduates of schools of education."

Patricia Biehl, a gifted and dedicated English teacher in a midwest high school, would agree with all that. But as I talked to her, it became increasingly clear that the objectives envisaged by all the reform reports are far from being accomplished. One hears in her voice the pain and anxiety and frustration of high school teachers throughout the nation. One also hears the voice of hope and dedication and, praise the Lord, of humor. But that voice is always haunted by the other voice, the voice that speaks, in her own metaphor, from the valley of death. Patty Biehl teaches in a suburban high school in central Ohio, a quintessentially mid-American kind of school, one might say, that is far from the agonized struggles of inner-city schools. If the cry for reform is so great there, I thought, what must it be in those schools that are less advantaged? One shudders to think.

BM—Is teaching high school as bad as everyone says it is?
PB—It depends on what you mean by bad.
BM—I mean bad in all senses of the word. I mean underpaid, unrewarding, bone wearying, and frustrating.
PB—For an English teacher, all of the above are true.
BM—Is it worse for English teachers?
PB—By the nature of the discipline, we see all the students. We are the only ones to do that, and our discipline requires that we teach them to read, to write, and to think. These are three separate charges we are expected to accomplish within a 50-minute period. Add to this preparation and correction time. If a teacher has an average load of 120 to 135 students, and it takes 10 minutes to correct a paper, you are talking about a 60 to 70 hour week. Definitely not ideal circumstances.
BM—I'd say downright bad.
PB—They are bad because we cannot do the job we know we could do if we had better working conditions.
BM—The same must be more or less true of the other disciplines as well.

PB—For the academic disciplines, yes, especially in schools where writing across the curriculum is required.

BM—Is writing across the curriculum any kind of solution?

PB—For the student it is; but it adds to the teachers' work load.

BM—Are most disciplines in high school academic?

PB—In a school like mine, about 50-50.

BM—Is the purpose of the nonacademic disciplines to track students?

PB—No, not exclusively. Tracking usually takes place in the individual disciplines, and in any event it begins in middle school. By the time students get to us, they are pretty well labeled. But at the high school level, there is a lot of crossover. For example, many of my honors students take nonacademic subjects, and they do it for different reasons: to get an easy A, to relieve the pressure, or simply because they are interested in the subject matter.

BM—If all disciplines shared the read-write-think responsibilities, would the situation improve?

PB—Not dramatically because we are facing something that is becoming more and more of a problem. Students are less and less prepared to do high school work.

BM—All educators seem to say that. I wonder if kindergarten teachers say their kiddies aren't prepared?

PB—I don't deny that things are bad up and down the line. But I have seen some convincing studies that show that there is as much as six years difference between 1965 and 1985 in the maturity level of beginning high school students. So you can imagine the problems that creates for the teacher.

BM—Where do you think the problem begins?

PB—I think students reflect the general values of society and of their parents in particular. We mouth a great respect for education in this country, but we really don't have much. Students have little or no respect for what we do. They don't really feel the need for what we have to offer. What they want are subjects that are relevant.

BM—Do they know what that means?

PB—No, but it boils down to a simplified career track. I am always amazed how career-oriented students are. If they don't know what they are going to do with the rest of their lives by age 18, they are extremely frustrated. A lot of this is encouraged by the guidance people who tell us that it's encouraged by the universities who tell us that it's encouraged by the parents who tell us that it is what society expects. So it becomes a vicious circle.

BM—Are you against tracking?

PB—It isn't the healthiest thing, I suppose. But what's the alternative? I certainly would rather teach a homogeneous group than a grab-bag of different kinds of students. That would be a teaching nightmare.

BM—What percentage of your students go to college?

PB—About 60 percent.

BM—Well above the national average.

PB—Oh, yes. Our school began as a predominantly rural institution and gradually took on a suburban character. So we have little middle. The students are either of a rural background and want basic nonacademic skills or they come from professional homes where their career aspirations are pegged higher. In either case, there is a commitment to finishing high school.

BM—So it is a better than average school?

PB—I think our offerings are very good. They are more than adequate to meet the requirements of college prep students, and we are well equipped to meet the needs of students who are not going to college. The problem is in the way the offerings are received, in the attitudes.

BM—We seem to have a conundrum here. On the one hand, report after report says that the public is dissatisfied with the quality of education and is demanding greater excellence in the schools. But what I hear you saying is that the public and particularly parents are the problem.

PB—The public is getting exactly what it wants from education.

BM—Is the public therefore hypocritical?

PB—Hypocrisy is as American as apple pie, and there are tons of it in our educational rhetoric. To be more charitable, I would say that the public is confused. It hasn't really thought through the question of what it wants from education. But it isn't hard to read between the lines. Parents don't want their children pressured. They don't want too much homework. The message we get is to teach what is necessary to succeed. And to complicate matters, we are now expected to teach about venereal disease, condoms, nutrition, family values, and interpersonal skills. I have been told over and over again by parents that it is far more important for their children to be socially adjusted than grade conscious. So I can't be too impressed by what the American public thinks or wants from education.

BM—That must give you a feeling of helplessness.

PB—That is perhaps the most frustrating aspect of the profession. If given an opportunity, high school teachers could lay out the educational conditions under which students could learn. We are never asked. We are part of a system that, by its very nature, dooms us to failure.

BM—Describe that system.

PB—The chain of command is pretty much the same in all public school systems. The public delegates the function of education to the government, which, in turn, delegates it to a local board. The school board delegates its authority to a superintendent, whose authority then trickles down to the principal and the teachers. The students aren't technically a part of the governing system at all. The idea behind this way of doing things was probably a good one. It was probably intended to ensure a broad base of representation through elections and the like. But what has resulted is an inefficient and inflexible bureaucracy. In practice, the superintendent holds most of the cards. The state only gets into the act at the level of broad (and minimal) policy issues.

BM—Popular wisdom has it that local control is one of the strengths of the American educational system.

PB—I have no problem with that.

BM—But you seem to be saying that the system is responsible for a lot of bad things.

PB—What I am complaining about is that no one at the state or the local level asks the teachers.

BM—So I am asking. I am your newly appointed superintendent, and I have a burning interest in what's on the minds of the teachers. So I come to you and I say, "Patty, what would you do to improve the system?"

PB—First, I would want academic faculty committees with real input into personnel and administrative decisions. At the very least, a veto power. I say academic faculty because the nonacademic programs have state-mandated rules and often state funds as well. So I would want two members from each of the academic departments, and I would want them to sit down and thrash out what is absolutely necessary for them to function well. Not adequately, but well. Then I would ask them to draw up an agenda to present to the administration.

BM—What would such a plan of action look like, say, for the

English department?

PB—First, a maximum of 20 students in any class that entails writing, and no more than four periods of teaching in an eight-period day. The average now is 30 to 35 students, and most faculty teach five or seven periods with one conference period. For an English teacher, that is impossible. I would recommend that we have two conference periods, one period of writing lab, and one planning period in which the staff is freed up to discuss its business. All we have now is a 30-minute lunch period in which to do our planning. I would also recommend that we cut out the crap factor.

BM—Which means?

PB—All the other stuff we have to do. Cafeteria duty—where we watch people chew. Hall monitoring—keeping the corridors safe for democracy, as we put it. Potty duty—we are supposed to keep the kids from fighting and smoking in the johns. To be reported for smoking, they have to be actually caught with a lighted cigarette in their mouths. The fact that the room is full of smoke does not constitute evidence. Also study hall duty—which can be particularly deterimental to the teaching role because we have to wear a different hat, resembling a prison warden's, and we tend to make enemies among the students. So when those students show up in your class later they are prejudiced from the study hall experience. Teachers shouldn't have to do that work.

BM—Who should?

PB—Paraprofessionals. Some schools have experimented with them, and it seems to work pretty well. Barring that, I think the administrators should do it. But they will tell you that they don't have the time. Moreover, they have the power to assign teachers to do it.

BM—What about parents?

PB—I am told that there are legal problems with that. Lack of certifications and so forth. And the same for volunteers.

BM—I would think it a natural role for the guidance people.

PB—But they are administrators, too.

BM—Tell me about the guidance business. That seems to loom large in American education. What do you think about it?

PB—I have respect for what they are supposed to do.

BM—What are they supposed to do?

PB—They are supposed to counsel the students in curriculum choices and career options. They also double as social workers to help kids with problems.

BM—Are they qualified to do this?

PB—They are certified.

BM—On the other hand, I can see a role with respect to psychological problems, especially with all the substance abuse around.

PB—That is in practice what happens with the juniors and seniors.

BM—On the other hand I can see a role with respect to psychological problems, especially with all the substance abuse around.

PB—I agree. The prevalence of drug use makes their role more crucial. But I wonder whether it ought to be done in the schools or not. I think other social agencies could do it better. I once had a student who used to set his hand on fire in class. On my inexpert diagnosis, he was a disturbed student. But it took four months to get him out of the classroom. The guidance counselors go by the book, and there are mounds of paperwork. There are so many roadblocks and so much buck passing that in many cases nothing gets done. Following the letter of the law doesn't seem to me to be the best way to deal with psychological problems.

BM—Well, I'm going to cast a sympathy vote for the counselors. I see it this way: You have before you, on the one hand, a raw mass of problem-ridden adolescents and, on the other, parents who have defected, an uncaring or uninformed public, overworked teachers, self-serving administrators, sclerotic social service agencies, and a confused clergy. The poor kids are caught in the middle, and the guidance people may be the only life line many of them have.

PB—I won't argue with that. But think about the educational implications here. You may have seen the movie *Teachers*. It caught some of the truth. But what struck me was that the lead character, who was supposed to be a teacher, did no teaching. He was a social worker. He dealt with problems students had. This is a very bad emphasis, but truly reflects the public's confused expectations that education should be therapy sessions. I resent that terribly. Our own school district is getting too heavily into that. Recently, we were convoked to discuss the goals and expectations of the district. What do we expect of our school system? To which I answered, "We have only one job, and it is to teach, and if we don't do that, we have no business here." That didn't go down too well. Someone objected that we must consider the whole child. I said, "I don't know what the whole child is, and even if I did, it's irrelevant. I am an English teacher." Someone asked me, "What do you do with disturbed children in your class?" I answered, "I get them out." I have 50 minutes to teach

English, and I am not a social worker. Somebody else suggested that we have to make a distinction between teaching versus learning. At that point, the jargon had set in, and my adrenalin started to rise. What I want to say and sometimes do is, "Don't give me the crap." When I use the word teach, I mean learn. That is what the word teach means, and it is not versus anything. What the jargon means, to the extent it means anything at all, is that students can't learn if they are on drugs, are sick, abused, or whatever. I don't deny that. But the public expectation is that we be refuges for the problem students. The only refuge I can give them is the refuge of the mind. I can teach them there is a way out of their situation, through the skills and knowledge I can impart. That's all I have to offer. I can give them a key that will open worlds. All they have to do is learn something. But I can tell you that jargonese is alive and well in my profession. I can give you dozens of examples. An administrator said one day, "We must give students the tools of learning." What does that man? Does it mean that English does not give them the tools? We must make them "life-long learners" is another one. To which I reply that you can't make them learners, life-long or otherwise, if you substitute therapy for hard requirements of the discipline. A colleague likes to say, "We must give the students confidence." I will accept that if it means giving them knowledge. Knowledge is power. Why are we so afraid of it? It's our trade. And we don't respect it. The saddest thing of all is that so many of our teachers don't respect the mind. I knew a principal once who said there was too much emphasis on academics. I said, "Not in this school there isn't." The latest buzz word is intervention. We are supposed to spot the problem kids in class and counsel them after school.

BM—*But I thought that was the job of counselors.*

PB—You would think so. But what happens is this: Problem kids don't do well. When they don't do well, the parents scream at the principal, whose natural instinct is to scream, in turn, at the teachers. Students aren't supposed to be failing, and if they are, it must be because teachers aren't doing their work. So we are told to intervene.

BM—*It certainly sounds unreasonable.*

PB—It's absurd in the full existential sense of the word. Worse, it is very insulting to the students themselves. We have armed them to the teeth with every excuse for not doing their work. They have all the excuses at their fingertips. "I had a headache." "My father didn't come home last night." "I couldn't do my homework because my mother locked me out." A big one is, "It's boring." Somehow that is supposed to count as a substantive reason for not doing work. Parents can be just as bad. One parent told me she understood why her son didn't like Shakespeare because she never liked Shakespeare. But, I said, it's not genetic. "I'm stressed out" is the latest cop out. Stated badly: Students come to us emotional and intellectual cripples and the system conspires to keep them that way.

BM—That's hitting hard.

PB—The harder the better.

BM—What is your own schedule like?

PB—I am at the school by 7:00 after a 20 or 25-minute drive. I begin teaching at 7:45. I teach five periods with one break. I have one conference period and teach one writing lab. I also direct the writing lab. I usually leave about 4:00, carrying two or three hours of work with me.

BM—It sounds like boot camp for the marines.

PB—It is a physically punishing schedule.

BM—When do you have time to think?

PB—Ha!

BM—It is inconceivable to most people how authoritarian that structure is. Moreso than most others in society, maybe including the marines.

PB—That is why most high school teachers laugh when we read the various reports blaming our failures. Teacher input into them is minimal to non-existent. The accountability issue is particularly bothersome. We are more than willing to be accountable. Our problem is that we don't want to be accountable for what we have no control over. Let us teach as we know how to teach. Give us a system in which we can teach.

BM—I'm looking as you talk at the members of the National Commission on Excellence in Education that produced the Nation at Risk *report.*

PB—How many teachers on it?

BM—One. A certain Jay Sommer who is listed as the National Teacher of the Year, 1981-82.

PB—How many non-teachers?

BM—Seventeen.

PB—I rest my case. When our system doesn't allow us to teach, and the public screams that the sorry state of education is our fault, it's ludicrous. We have no direct control over anything in our professional lives. I have always worked in a system that "allows" us to set our curriculum and staff our department. But I underline the word allow. The administrators retain the power. And the day they do not wish to allow our participation, it's over.

BM—Who does the hiring?

PB—The superintendent.

BM—Not the principal?

PB—No. He is an advisor.

BM—Do faculty advise?

PB—Some of them. Sometimes. It depends on the principal.

BM—Is there no way around this system?

PB—Any way around is called insubordination for which you can be fired, even if you are on a continuing contract.

BM—So no one bucks the system?

PB—No.

BM—Would you say this is the root of the morale problem?

PB—Absolutely. If you want to walk through the valley of death, visit a high school.

BM—But you don't have to contend with the problems of the inner-city schools.

PB—They are worse. But it is bad everywhere, at least where morale is concerned.

BM—High schools always remind me of minimal security institutions.

PB—But the work goes on. That has to be said. I work with the most dedicated group of teachers I can imagine. My department gives hours and hours of time, well beyond what they are being paid for or, for that matter, what is expected of them. So we don't like it much when the reports rap our knuckles for what we aren't doing.

BM—The reports hit on the administrators, too.

PB—They do. But the administrators have more power and are better able to defend themselves. And few administrator are going to put the teachers' interest before their own. I will say, however, that I have always been backed by administrators in discipline cases.

BM—Would you say better salaries would go some distance to solving your problems?

PB—In addition to some of the other recommendations I would make, yes.

BM—What would be a good starting salary for a high school teacher?

PB—The same as the starting salary for a doctor, lawyer, or engineer. Somewhere between 25 and 30 thousand a year. We delude ourselves when we think that teaching is not as important as any other profession and that it ought not be proportionately rewarded.

BM—We've always appealed to idealism to justify the teaching profession.

PB—Not any more. Idealism was a code word which meant women who were willing to work for peanuts. Women aren't willing to do that anymore. The average career of a high school teacher today is between three and five years.

BM—How long have you been teaching?

PB—Thirteen years.

BM—Will you stay the course?

PB—I expect I will.

BM—What keeps teachers in the game?

PB—When it works, there is nothing like it. The greatest thing in the world is to see students begin to think, to tackle a problem and figure it out, to see something they never saw before. One of my prim and proper conservative students came up to me the other day and said, "Ms. Biehl, I don't like your class." I asked why. She said, "Because it always unsettles me." I knew then that I was doing good teaching.

BM—Does this happen often enough to enough teachers to sustain them?

PB—No, it doesn't.

BM—Then I repeat my previous question: What keeps them in the game?

PB—Many who stay in become routinized. It's a job. They leave at 3:00 and take no work with them. And, in all honesty, that is all the public is paying for. Not one thing more. Those who give more are considered stupid. Those who give the minimum are smart.

BM—So we are back to the morale problem?

PB—Yes, teachers are frustrated, angry, powerless in their own profession, and eventually cynical. Yet we receive all the blame for the failures of education, beginning with our own administrators.

BM—Do you sometimes think another two years in graduate school for the Ph. D. and a college career might not have been a wise decision?

PB—My students sometimes ask me that. I guess I would have been happier. And I know many of my colleagues would have been happier. No question about it. But deep down, I have to say that, all things being equal, I would rather be where I am.

BM—But things aren't equal.

PB—That is why it is so frustrating.

BM—You have formidable enemies: your students, your administrators, parents, the great unwashed public. What about your own professional associations? Are you well served by them?

PB—Very poorly. The Ohio Educational Association just went into the red by several hundred thousand dollars.

BM—Where do they spend their money?

PB—Who knows? My guess is that they have the same problem most bureaucracies do. They are top heavy in administration and terribly mismanaged. So next year we may have to pay them 35 dollars more a year in dues.

BM—What does the NEA do for you?

PB—I haven't found that out yet.

BM—What is the best thing you can say about your professional associations?

PB—In the early eighties the Ohio Educational Association got collective bargaining for us. This means that the districts have to bargain with the teachers on salaries. I have been part of that process several times, and it can get very nasty. We never get what we want, but I'll be the first to say it's better that the previous system which amounted to the teacher telling the principal how much she wanted and the principal telling her how much he would give her.

BM—That sounds like a significant gain.

PB—We have made substantial gains in our contractual arrangements, but not in academic matters. And I suspect that we are going to have to put into the contract what we want for the curriculum. But there are disadvantages in doing it that way because what we put in a contract can bind us as well as help us. We need flexibility to do what is necessary to do to teach well.

BM—What is necessary to teach well? I read recently that something like 85 percent of high school work is rote memory.

PB—I don't know where that figure came from. But I'll say this in defense of memory: If we don't have it, we don't have the basic building blocks of knowledge. I think we have denigrated memory too much. As a consequence, students don't know any facts; they don't have any historical knowledge; they lack the basic cultural information any educated person should have. Now I agree that memory is not all of education. But it is an important part. Moreover, it is not the role of the high schools to teach memory skills. These should be mastered by the end of the eighth grade. Try running a Socratic discussion with students who lack facts. It devolves into a matter if feeling. Students think the "I feel" is a clincher in any argument. When they come up against someone else's "I feel," they shrug and conclude that everything is relative.

BM—Is your best teaching with honors students?

PB—No question about it.

BM—And the rest is drudgery?

PB—Not all of it. Freshmen, yes. That is the real scut work in high schools, not only because they are so unprepared academically, but they lack basic discipline and etiquette as well.

BM—The lion-taming factor.

PB—Preferably with a whip and chair. And it has to be done. But I have good courses other than APs. One of my favorites is a junior course called Accent. It's for non-college preps, and for most of them, it's the last English course these students will ever see. For some of them, the first. They lack minimal skills in reading and have no interest in English, but they have to take it.

BM—So what makes it enjoyable?

PB—Well, these kids have made up their minds that they are not going to be bored. So they want to discuss everything. Of course, they have no facts to base a discussion on. But with patience, I find I can teach them a few, and they are some of the best participators I have.

BM—Do high school teachers still flunk students?

PB—I do. In fact, I have one of the highest failure rates. That's why I don't teach freshmen anymore. I flunked as many as 50 percent of the class. But my department in general are hard graders. And we catch holy hell from the administration. This reflects badly on the system, and administrators say it reflects bad teaching. If we were good teachers, they say, our students would pass. Students have the same idea in their heads. "But I tried," they say.

BM—To which you respond?

PB—You didn't master the material.

BM—All of this is part of the consumer mentality that has infected the teaching profession. Here is an interesting tidbit I noticed in the paper the other day, which claims the problem with schools is that they should be run on a business model. The item reads: "Imagine a company that has little quality control, churns out shoddy products,

*and then wants more money; imagine a company that gets millions of
dollars from stockholders, has virtually no competition, and yet ends
up bankrupt; imagine a company that takes a decade and $40,000 to
churn out each product then somehow loses up to half of these
products before delivery. . . ." And on it goes.*

PB—I suppose the imagined business is the public schools.
BM—Right. What do you say to that kind of criticism?
PB—I say I am not turning out cars, and the analogy is a false one.
It would be like modeling education on sports, which is another false
analogy we often hear.
BM—We should talk about sports.
PB—I have never seen much educational value to sports, except as
intramural. I think it is a concession to the peculiar American insist-
ance that education be entertaining.
*BM—Corruption these days seems to enter academe most
frequently through the athletic department. But you and I are not
going to be able to do much about it. So let's move on. I want to ask
you a question about teacher training. Isn't that another of the
formidable obstacles to effective teaching?*
PB—The problem is that high school teachers are taught by university professors. Most of them don't have direct experience in high
school classrooms. The methods courses, and they are the only ones
that make any sense at all, are not taught by practicing high school
teachers. They should be. So we have a very real problem here.
*BM—What would you consider the best preparation for a high
school teacher?*
PB—Extensive study in a major area, a good liberal arts
education. A teacher needs to know a subject area in order to have
something to teach.
BM—Would you abolish the education major?
PB—Yes. Education as such has no subject matter.
BM—What about the craft itself?
PB—I am not sure that can be taught. One can learn some things
about it, but it is mostly a combination of native talent and practice. I
have never heard a teacher in any discipline say anything good about
education training.
BM—Did you learn anything?
PB—Absolutely nothing. It was a waste of time from beginning to
end. I learned how to teach by observing the good teachers I had. It's
something you assimilate. Ironically, all the reforms we've had have

had the effect of adding more educational requirements, thus compounding the problem. An undergraduate education major is like a pre-med major in that both leave little time for anything else.

BM—The question that has been lurking in the back of my mind for a while now is the civics question. We are supposed to be educating for democracy. What do you do with that?

PB—We have to teach students to think. Not what to think, but how to think. That is all I can do. And all I should do. Furthermore, if I do it well, I have done a very important thing for democracy.

BM—That sometimes gets labeled the elitist position.

PB—Well, if that is the case, I happen to think elitism can be a good thing. At any rate, it doesn't have to be a bad thing. Bear in mind, too, that other agencies have important roles in educating for democracy. Schools can't do it all, although, as I indicated, they can do an important part of it. We commit hubris when we assign the major responsibility to the schools. Americans want the schools to do everything. I might say here, too, that I think a half day of high school is enough, five periods. In the remaining time, teachers can do some of their important work, and students can engage in a variety of extracurricular activities like work and sports and other citizen-forming endeavors. I think it is wrong and counterproductive to bottle them up for the whole day in the classroom. And that is not an elistist position.

BM—Touché. Some states are considering adding more days to the school year, including Ohio. I suppose you would be against that.

PB—Certainly.

BM—Who is the best student you have ever had?

PB—That's a tough one.

BM—Let me rephrase that question, and ask you to describe an ideal high school student, a composite profile if you will.

PB—As I think about it, three things seem absolutely necessary: a desire to learn, the ability to learn, and the discipline to learn. Ability doesn't mean intelligence exactly, or at least need not. I have good students who weren't exceptionally intelligent by the usual standards, but they had the hunger and they worked and they went on to do well. Give me students with these qualities, and all my dreams come true. Then I can give them what I have to give, which is knowledge. That is what I can share. And that is when teaching is fun. I tell the bored students that learning won't be much fun until they master the basics, so we can ascend to a level where the sparks do fly.

BM—How important do you think verbal skills are?

PB—Very important.

BM—I have noticed a problem with honors students at the college level. Many of them are surprisingly tongue-tied. My own theory is that in order to get to be an honors student in the American system, you have to be a good tester. And to be a good tester, you generally have to keep your mouth shut and memorize. This breeds an intellectually timid student, one not sensitive to the drama of ideas, not at ease with the give and take of ideas. What do you think?

PB—I don't define a good student as a good test taker.

BM—But unless they are, they aren't going to get far in the academic game.

PB—True. And I tell them that. It may not be fair, but that's the way it is. But there is more, much more. To an extent, you have to teach to the tests, to the SATs and the like. I am no great lover of tests like that, but they do serve as a carrot to spur students to do what they otherwise wouldn't do. And they are good predictors of college performance.

BM—But that is self-referential. All it says is that if students do well at one stage of the system, they are likely to do well at a later stage. It says nothing about the system itself.

PB—I agree. And the tests tell you nothing about the disciplinary habits of the students. I have had kids with scores in the 1400s who failed my course because they didn't do the work. Some of my students have missed out on scholarships and admission to good universities for that reason. Also, tests don't tell you much about thinking ability. I've found that a lot of good testers are not good thinkers. They are regurgitators. I've also noticed that good students tend to want to please. They do well on tests to please the teacher. That kind of student is lost in an open-ended discussion. They will wait for everyone else to give an opinion, and then they want to know what the teacher thinks. If they should disagree with you, they are very apologetic. That, I think, is a comment on a kind of authoritarian teaching that expects the one right answer. Such students have prospered under that system and so aren't inclined to question it. One attempt to deal with this problem is a proliferation of critical thinking courses. They are the in thing now. But, like education courses, they should not be free-standing. To think critically is inherent in a subject matter.

BM—What changes do you see from the reforms we hear so much about?

PB—There is a paradox here. I don't think the whole system has to be reformed. A few sound, piecemeal adjustments of the sort I have described would go a long way. But the minute you change the system at one point, the whole structure threatens to come tumbling down like a house of cards. So the bureaucrats are, in that sense, smart to prevent any significant reform at all. They are out there at the end of the whip which, once cracked, will send them flying. The system as it is now runs on its own momentum and disallows interference. So no one, either at the top or the bottom, is capable of undertaking serious reform.

BM—A final question. I've been wanting to ask it for a long time. Why don't high school teachers rise up in the moral equivalent of armed revolution?

PB—Sometimes I ask myself the same question. But I have indicated a partial answer. Teachers are part of a self-propelling system. They are in it not because they want to change it, but, on the contrary, because they are comfortable with it. As students, they did well and liked the authoritarian structure. So now they perpetuate it.

BM—I need something more upbeat for a conclusion.

PB—Teachers are not by nature aggressive. But I do know that they care. They care about the students, their intellectual development, and their future. Individual teachers are not often aware of the total problem. Communication among teachers as professionals is almost nonexistent. I regret that we do not have better working conditions. And I think it is somehow unfair that the burden of improving those conditions rests primarily upon our own shoulders. My best guess is that when teachers as a professional group become aware that the system is actually damaging the very students they are there to help, they will take action.

BM—Let's hope so. Thank you very much. □

An Interview with
DEREK BOK on

Teaching Ethics

IT is emerging with alarming clarity that the baseline question for higher education in the receding years of this century is how to educate for civic competence. That we have missed the boat on this is a national tragedy and a cynical gloss on the design of democracy. The charge, flatly stated, is that the value neutrality that undergirds our prevailing philosophies of education has obelized civic education as a worthy end of our efforts. When in the mid-eighties, I was thinking about this problem and casting about in my mind for someone who might offer a convincing counterargument, I thought of Derek Bok, the president of Harvard University. He had been wrestling with similar questions in a number of speeches and articles and had just written a book on the social responsibilities of the university. When I journeyed to the Harvard campus to talk to Bok, he told me that the charge had some truth to it. But he quickly added, "We ought not think that everyone in academia is in the grip of an evil positivism, or that all professors are uninterested in the public purposes of education. I have never subscribed to the view that education is narrowly limited to intellectual pursuits or has no responsibility for the social conscience of its students. That is a shriveled view of education, and I reject it."

I was glad to hear him say that. But then Bok went on to make a distinction that was less heartening. The distinction, he said, is between the university as a corporate entity and the individuals who comprise it. "Anyone in the university is free to take any position he or she wants to, and they can do it individually or collectively. That is the point of academic freedom. My argument is that the institution cannot take such positions." I objected that many would consider that position a dodge. Bok admitted that universities are caught uncomfortably between their ideals, which tend to be of a transcendent and timeless nature, and the necessity to exist in and serve the practical shorter-range goals of society. "The activist argument is very strong," Bok admitted. "There are a lot of people out there who believe in the university militant, and they make the point very persuasively that there are a lot of problems in the world that demand urgent attention and the university cannot afford to stand back."

He went on to state his position from another angle. "In doing their proper work," he said, "universities provide significant public goods and educate the public in a wide variety of ways. We ought not mystify the notion of civic education to the point that it can be done only by special people in special ways under special circumstances. It is a far less esoteric process. One of the great public acts of our history was the creation of the land grant university and the multi-university that subsequently emerged. They inculcate literacy; they are responsible for professional training; they provide new knowledge through research and make it useful through the professions. These are all high-order social values that any democracy must cherish and encourage. Citizens can't communicate until they have learned communication skills; they can't influence policymakers until they have grasped some body of knowledge; they can't function effectively as citizens unless they have some historical grasp of their political culture. Moreover, our faculty and faculty at other universities write frequently for the general press, serve in consulting roles, take government positions, and undertake other activities that all have at least the *indirect* outcome of giving citizens a greater stake in the polity."

With these words, Bok provided a substantial part of the counterargument I was seeking. Another part was supplied by some remarks he made about the teaching of ethics. He alluded to an article he had written on the subject in 1976, in which he argued that the teaching of ethics was a necessary arm of education and essential to the quality of our social life. The question of civic education began to take shape in my mind, as I thought it was in Bok's mind, as a subset of the more radical problem of educating for ethical responsibility. I could see that civic competence was an ethical obligation, a part of what it means to be a moral being. Some philosophers have argued that point, but not much recently. So, to think of the civic problem, one had to think of the ethical problem, and that approach brings us abruptly up against the bleak underside of our affluent society. We seem to be confronted with a triple combination of unprecedented ethical problems in the public sphere, a high incidence of immoral conduct on the part of political leaders, and some lamentable foot dragging on the part of educators. Bok is preeminent among those who believe that ethics is central to our educational efforts. He has, moreover, taken a number of initiatives at his own institution that have proven exemplary for others. In what follows, he sets forth his latest thinking on the subject.

BM—Ethics seems to have become a cottage industry in academia today. Why do you think that is the case?

DB—For one thing, revelations about the conduct of prominent public figures like Ivan Boesky, Jim Bakker, Oliver North, Michael Deaver, and others have prompted fresh concern over the standards of behavior exhibited by influential people in our society. Their conduct has dramatized, if you will, the need to rethink our ethical convictions.

BM—Do you think the concern for ethics indicates one of those seismic shifts in public opinion that every now and again overtakes the American people?

DB—That may well be the case. During most of the twentieth century, first artists and intellectuals, then broader segments of the society challenged every convention, every prohibition, every regulation that cramped the human spirit or blocked its appetites and ambitions. Today, a reaction has set in, born of a recognition that the public needs common standards to hold a diverse society together, to prevent ecological diaster, to maintain confidence in government, to conserve scarce resources, to escape disease, to avoid the inhumane applications of technology. This new respect for limits is likely to carry with it a concern for the moral values and restraints that unify communities and keep human conduct within acceptable bounds.

BM—Judging from your writings and frequent public speeches on the issue, you clearly think universities have a special role in shaping the moral consciousness of society.

DB—Yes, I do. Almost every public servant, business executive, attorney, physician—indeed, virtually all leaders in every walk of life—enter our colleges and professional schools and remain there for several formative years. Other institutions in society also play an important role in the development of young people—especially families, schools, and communities of faith. But only a minority of children now grow up in a two-parent family, and the time they spend with adults of any kind has been dropping steadily for several decades. Schools are often preoccupied with problems of racial integration, political intervention, drugs, and strikes while suffering the effects of a long-term decline in the status of teachers. Religious institutions no longer seem as able as they once were to impart basic values to the young. In these circumstances, universities need to think hard about what they can do in the face of what many perceive as a widespread decline in ethical standards.

BM—How ethical do you think students are?

DB—Several studies have found that undergraduates are growing less altruistic and more preoccupied with self-serving goals. In polls of entering freshmen over the past 15 to 20 years, the values that have risen most are the desire to be "very well-off financially," to gain personal recognition, and to have administrative responsibility for the work of others. The goal that has plummeted furthest is the desire to find "a meaningful philosophy of life." Other values that have fallen include the desire to keep up to date in political affairs, to participate in community action programs, and to help clean up the environment. Further studies suggest that the number of college students who admit to having cheated in class has risen appreciably over the past 30 years. So I see some problems here.

BM—Of course, universities traditionally have had as part of their mission the development of a moral sense and the formation of character.

DB—Until the twentieth century that was the case. As Plato said: "If you ask what is the good of education, the answer is easy—that education makes good men, and that good men act nobly." In the New World, Harvard was founded to prepare ministers of upright character. By the eighteenth century, the college had added moral philosophy to Bible study—to the consternation of Cotton Mather— but the principal aim was still to develop "good men," or in Jefferson's words, "an aristocracy of talent and virtue." These tendencies continued strongly into the nineteenth century. Indeed, a Massachusetts law passed in 1789 and reaffirmed in 1826 made Harvard's priorities clear: "The president, professors and tutors of the University at Cambridge . . . shall exert their best endeavors to impress on the minds of children and youth committed to their care and instruction the principles of piety and justice and a sacred regard for truth, love of their country, humanity and universal benevolence, sobriety, industry and frugality, chastity, moderation and temperance, and those other virtues which are the ornament of human society and the basis upon which a republican constitution is founded." Furthermore, these exhortations were backed by elaborate codes of conduct that were in turn backed by fines, demerits, and even expulsion.

BM—Why did this function of education fall into eclipse?

DB—Well, that's a long and pretty familiar story. If I were to pick a cause among many causes, I would say the publication of Darwin's *The Origin of Species* in 1859. That had the effect of undermining religion, which traditionally has been the chief agent of moral instruction, and of introducing a new academic ethos. There was a time when Harvard graded students on their conduct, but that practice was abandoned in 1869. There was a time when we looked at personal character in considering candidates for faculty appointment. We haven't done that for a long time. Intellect and technical proficiency have decisively triumphed as the preeminent goals of the professoriat.

BM—Couldn't that change of emphasis be read as the introduction of a new ethics rather than the abandonment of ethics?

DB—It has been interpreted that way. In fact, it was interpreted that way by Harvard's famous "Redbook," *General Education in a Free Society*, which stated that "the best way to infect the student with the zest for intellectual integrity is to put him near a teacher who is himself selflessly devoted to truth." This was in effect an endorsement of the Socratic dictum that knowledge of the good will lead to doing good.

BM—Do you believe that?

DB—There is scant evidence for it. Socrates sometimes talked as if knowledge alone would suffice to ensure virtuous action. He did not stress the value of early habituation, positive example, and obedience to rules in giving students the desire and self-discipline to live up to their beliefs and to respect the basic norms of behavior essential to civilized communities.

BM—If 1859 was the beginning of the decline, when would you date the renewal of interest in ethics?

DB—Late in the 1960s. Amid the turmoil of those protest-ridden years, new problems emerged to rivet the public mind on ethical questions. Prominent among them were such issues as abortion, race relations, and affirmative action. As interest mounted around the country, moral philosophers, theologians, law professors, and sociologists began to express their opinions in newspaper columns and scholarly journals. A new academic concern for practical ethics had emerged. Gradually, courses appeared in college and professional school catalogues on ethical questions. Interestingly, medicine led the way even though its academic disciplines and scientific ethos were farthest removed of all the professional schools from moral philosophy. Ethical problems simply became too pressing to ignore. The tumult over abortion was quickly joined by a host of other controversies: when to allow terminal patients to die, whether to permit "test-tube" babies, what standards to apply in performing medical experiments on human beings. Suddenly, hospitals saw their practices criticized in newspaper articles while doctors had to defend themselves in court. Confronted with these perils, medical deans reached out to philosophers, priests, lawyers, and whomever else they could find to lecture their students on medical ethics.

BM—And it spread from medical ethics to other professions?

DB—With minor variations, yes. As controversies arose over political scandals, business fraud, engineering catastrophies, and fictitious newspaper stories, courses on ethics made their way into schools of business, public administration, engineering, and journalism. In law schools, following the revelations of Watergate, the American Bar Association persuaded the deans to agree to make instruction on professional responsibility a requirement for admission to the bar. In colleges, too, offerings in practical ethics and moral reasoning began to appear.

BM—Are we talking about a success story here?

DB—I wouldn't put it that way. Ethics is firmly established in the curriculum but it still faces considerable obstacles.

BM—For example?

DB—I distinguish between the internal and the external obstacles. Internally, there has been faculty skepticism. A decade ago, there was concern that applied ethics was a soft subject that would fall into the hands of ideologues bent on forcing their views upon students. These fears have receded with experience. A more troublesome problem, however, is the dearth of well-trained faculty to offer instruction, especially in professional schools. Courses in professional ethics are difficult to teach because they call for preparation in two entirely different subjects: moral philosophy (or a related discipline) and some area of practical application, such as government, law, business, or medicine. Since no established program in a university combines training in both fields, instructors typically have to teach themselves an important part of what they need to know. Such preparation can often be inadequate, causing instruction to be irritatingly superficial or theoretical.

BM—What are the external obstacles?

DB—I am thinking of the criticisms from some prominent neoconservatives, like former Secretary of Education William Bennett. These critics claim that teachers of practical ethics are so anxious to be tolerant of differing ethical systems and creeds that they lead students to believe that all moral views are entitled to equal respect. Neoconservatives also assert that instructors try too hard not to engage in indoctrination, even to the point of refusing to endorse such basic virtues as honesty and keeping one's word. Finally, teachers of applied ethics are attacked for emphasizing difficult moral dilemmas that seem to have no convincing solution, thus leaving the impression that all questions of morality are unanswerable. Because of these shortcomings, critics claim that courses in practical ethics, at best, will confuse students, reinforce their ethical relativism, and fail to improve their standards of behavior. At worst, it is said, participants will emerge from such classes more cynical about ethics and cleverer at thinking up plausible arguments for any course of conduct they wish to follow.

BM—Could you devise an ideal curriculum to overcome these obstacles?

DB—Not an ideal curriculum, which probably doesn't exist. But I do have some ideas. One of the big questions is whether we should offer special courses on ethics or whether we should emphasize the ethical component of every course. I think both alternatives have merit. Certainly the traditional liberal arts curriculum helps in many ways to develop ethical awareness and moral reasoning. Literature and history, courses in the sciences and social sciences, all provide opportunities to develop ethical awareness and moral reasoning. The same is true of courses in the professional schools. At the same time, without courses specifically devoted to moral problems, there will be no one to teach the subject in depth, no one to carry on sustained writing in the field, no one to whom other faculty members can turn for advice on how to deal with ethical questions arising in their own courses. Under such conditions, efforts to insert ethical issues into the regular curriculum will almost certainly wither. A wise faculty, therefore, will seek to provide both special courses in applied ethics and opportunities to discuss moral problems as they emerge in other subjects throughout the curriculum. But, however good a curriculum we come up with, we have to go beyond the classroom if we are going to influence behavior.

BM—Talk more about that.

DB—We have to make a total institutional effort. To begin with, universities have to have rules that prohibit violation of fundamental moral norms like lying and cheating, and these rules must be administered fairly and consistently with penalities sufficient to make the rules credible. But moral responsibility cannot develop through rules and penalties alone. It must grow out of a genuine concern for others and a desire to respect their legitimate interests. The best way of acquiring such concern is to experience situations in which one can appreciate the effects of one's actions on others and understand how one's own interests are affected in return. Education does not automatically provide enough of these experiences. So I urge that there be more extracurricular activities that stress collaborative and communal relationships.

BM—Like what?

DB—I think community service programs are especially valuable because they offer such a vivid opportunity to perceive the needs of others while feeling the satisfaction of helping people less fortunate than oneself. Such programs are all the more important today in light of the 15-year trend among college students toward valuing self-centered aspirations at the expense of more altruistic goals. To encourage these activites, universities should encourage them publicly, offer seed money to help them get started, and assist in their administration and supervision. Professional schools might even offer further incentives by giving positive weight to applications from students who have devoted substantial time and effort to endeavors of this kind. In recent years, universities have been doing more to encourage community service. More than 100 institutions have joined a new organizaton, Campus Compact, to stimulate the growth of such activities. Yet community service still does not receive the support it deserves from American colleges. Only a minority of campuses have sponsored programs of this kind, and only a small fraction of the student body is typically involved. Moreover, most institutions that have programs do not give them the level of support or supervision commonly offered even to minor athletic sports. The final point I would make is that the moral climate of the university as an institution must send the right messages. Universities periodically encounter moral problems in the course of investing their stock, interacting with the surrounding community, implementing affirmative action, and carrying out other tasks. The way in which they address these issues will not be lost upon their students. Nothing is so likely to produce cynicism, especially among those taking courses in practical ethics, as a realization that the very institution that offers such classes shows little concern for living up to its own moral obligations.

BM—Do you think sports are a good influence on students?

DB—Yes, because coaches can have such a powerful effect on their players and because varsity athletics constantly present sharp conflicts between ends and means. Alas, few universities with "big-time" programs have done much to prepare their coaches to address moral problems, or even to convince them that winning is not the most important criterion for judging their performance. Even so, many coaches do manage to set a good ethical example for their teams. Many others have subjected their players to a long list of dubious maneuvers to gain a competitive edge: allowing unauthorized scrimmages to occur, encouraging an excessively violent style of play, keeping star athletes eligible even when they misbehave, committing petty recruiting violations. The persistence of these transgressions and the willingness of campus authorities to overlook them send a damaging message to students about how important ethical standards are when they conflict with intense ambitions to succeed.

BM—When we get to the role of coaches, aren't we getting pretty close to indoctrination?

DB—Nothing I have mentioned should compromise the university's obligation to respect the freedom of every student to express any opinion or entertain any view on moral as well as political, social, and aesthetic questions. This is why particular religious doctrines, however important they may be in guiding the ethical beliefs of individual students, can never be adopted by a secular university as the basis for its program of moral education. What the institution can do is to offer arguments and encouragement of various kinds to persuade students to adhere to basic ethical norms. These norms—honesty, nonviolence, promise keeping, respect for property, and other legitimate interests—are all so fundamental and so universal that they have proved essential to virtually every civilized society. As a result, institutional efforts encouraging students to act according to these precepts should not give justifiable offense to any campus group, even in the most diverse student body.

BM—Suppose we had in place everything you recommend; would we improve the moral lives of our students?

DB—We have to be cautious in our claims. A university is only one institution among many that affect students' lives. It offers an experience late in youth when ideas and values are more developed and students less open to adult advice than in earlier years. It competes with television, motion pictures, and the tumult of an outside world replete with scandals and lurid exposés. With its commitment to intellectual freedom and diversity, a university even lacks the power to bring a consistent, coordinated influence to bear on those who live and work within its walls. For many students, its efforts to communicate on moral questions will be all but lost amid the distractions of the countless groups and extracurricular activities that fill the typical campus. Although these difficulties are real, we can still say the universities play an important role in helping students define their ethical responsibilities. The moral environment of the university teaches tolerance, a respect for differing values, a recognition of the complexity of human problems. In doing so, it prepares students well for the real world and helps a perceptive person to acquire a moral understanding far richer and more firmly rooted in the intricacies of modern life than simpler dogmas nurtured in more homogeneous, more carefully controlled environments. With their classes, their residential halls, their extracurricular activities, and extensive counseling services, colleges and universities have created a world that dominates the lives and thoughts of countless people during years in which their character and values are being formed. Under these conditions, students must get help from their universities in developing moral standards or they are unlikely to get much assistance at all.

BM—That sounds like a lot. But is it enough?

DB—No, I think we are far from making an adequate, let alone a maximum, effort. Some efforts are being made on every campus, of course, and a number of religious institutions and small independent colleges actually devote much time and energy to the task. More often, however, and especially in large universities, the subject is not treated as a serious responsibility worthy of sustained discussion and determined action by the faculty and administration.

BM—Who has the primary responsibility in spearheading this effort?

DB—If the situation is to change, I have no doubt where the initiative must lie. Universities will never do much to encourage a genuine concern for ethical issues or to help their students to acquire a strong and carefully considered set of moral values unless presidents and deans take the lead. Without their endorsement and example, the diffidence and inertia that dog the subject of moral responsibility will continue to keep these issues at the margin of everyday campus life.

BM—Does this consign the faculty to a secondary role?

DB—Not at all. I said the initiative lies with presidents and deans. But an equal responsibility rests with the faculty. More than any other group, they set the tone of the institution and establish what is important, what is legitimate, what truly merits the time and attention of the students. Unless professors recognize the importance of moral education, unless they personally participate by treating ethical issues in their classes, counseling students, helping to define and administer rules of behavior on campus, any effort along these lines will lack credibility and force. Indeed, without such involvement, scholarly traditions of value-free inquiry may foster a sense among students and administrators that ethical questions are private matters to be kept out of serious conversation.

BM—Would you put moral education on a par with research and professional training as an aim of the modern university?

DB—I'll answer with one of my favorite quotations. It's from Montaigne who said: "To compose our character is our duty, not to compose books, and to win, not battles and provinces, but order and tranquility in our own conduct. Our great and glorious masterpiece is to live appropriately."

BM—That's a meaty quote. We'll ponder it. □

An Interview with
DANIEL CALLAHAN on

Applying the Humanities

A GOOD portion of the intellectual work of our society is carried out
by think tanks. These comprise centers, institutes, and foundations
of all hues and colors that function for the most part outside of the
normal educational establishments. Preeminent among these is the
Hastings Center, which takes its name from the tree-lined town on
the Hudson River which was for many years its home.

The Hastings Center was cofounded in 1969 by Daniel Callahan,
who was at the time a freshly-minted Ph.D. in philosophy from
Harvard University. He continues to serve as director. The center's
initial interest was in biomedical ethics. That remains an important
emphasis, but the center has expanded in recent years to study
problems in the fields of the behavioral sciences, public policy, and
applied and professional ethics. "In the early days of our work,"
Callahan says, "there was a great interest in individual moral decisions and in the exotica of biomedical research like cloning. Recently
the focus has moved from concerns of the individual toward more
comprehensive decisions made by and affecting larger groups of
people. This change is a direct result of a contemporary shift in the
way professions like medicine, law, and journalism are being practiced. This raises serious ethical problems."

Thus, in the late seventies, the Hastings Center published a widely
heralded series of monographs on the teaching of ethics in higher

education. Decisions concerning health care allocations are typical of the kind of problem the center deals with, and Callahan recently published a controversial book advocating that such allocations be limited for the elderly. All the professions are turning up ethical dilemmas of an unprecedented sort. "In the case of law," Callahan says, "it is increasingly recognized that, however important the interests of the client, there can also be other interests—justice, fairness, and the integrity of our system of law. And in journalism, vying with the public's right to know is the right of citizens to privacy, to confidentiality, and to their personal reputations." When asked about the moral temperature of the country, Callahan answers that the realm of morality is never black or white. That inherent ambiguity is further compounded by the diminishing moral authority of religion. Still, Callahan, says, "I am optimistic that there is a greater possibility of moral consensus than there was in the past."

When I interviewed him in 1986, he had just coauthored a book entitled *Applying the Humanities*. That seemed like the opportune subject to get our conversation going.

BM—Why did you decide to do a book on the humanities?
DC—The idea for the project came from a couple of sources. Most immediately it came from our own work here at the Hastings Center where we have been trying to take the humanities to the sciences, to use the methods and perspectives of the humanities to deal with issues primarily in medicine and biology but occasionally in science more generally. It has been obvious to us ever since we started that there were big problems in this approach. After all, there aren't many precedents for this sort of thing. And, of course, there was great suspicion on the part of the scientific community who wondered just what, if anything, we had to offer. Another source for the project was the general discussion during the sixties and into the seventies about the role of the humanities, the future of the humanities, the relevance of the humanities, etc. It was a lively discussion and we got caught up in that.
BM—Has that larger discussion faded?
DC—It certainly isn't as strong as it was. There has been in the last decade a lot of commotion on the educational front, various curriculum reforms and reports, which have attempted to give a more central role to the humanities. On the other hand, the curriculum has become much more professionalized with emphasis

on career tracks like business and law. I don't know where the focus of that discussion is now. Maybe it has run out of gas, as often happens to debates of this kind. But we think discussion about the humanities ought to go on.

BM—Do you feel that your book landed in a kind of void?

DC—As I analyze the situation of the humanities at the present time, there is on the one hand a return to a strong sense of disciplinary integrity. Research and scholarship in the humanities is as strong, or stronger, than it has ever been, and in the universities this is very important for purposes of tenure and promotion. At the other end of the spectrum, there is a great investment of manpower in remedial work at the entry level. What seems to us missing is the work in between, where the humanities relate to other disciplines and have some impact on society. I don't know whether it is true or not, but I have the impression that a polarization between highly specialized and broadly remedial work has taken place in the humanities.

BM—It is certainly true to some extent. On the other hand, there seems to be a good deal of applied stuff going on. By your own account, medical ethics is strong. So is business ethics. And there are many courses dealing with science and society, all of which have some applied content.

DC—Some of this may be a hangover from an earlier period. The conservative turn at the National Endowment for the Humanities and other humanities organizations does not favor the kind of work we are doing. NEH, especially when Bill Bennett was its chairman, made it pretty clear that they were interested in getting back to basic work with the great books.

BM—Speaking of that, your book seems in part a polemic against the kind of position espoused by Bennett and his cohorts.

DC—Maybe not a polemic exactly. I think that debate got confused. To the extent that Bennett was saying that people not well grounded in the humanities to begin with shouldn't use them to provide instant solutions to social problems, I agree with him. But I think Bennett was claiming much more. He was saying that the humanities have no business engaging in social problems at any level, that the humanities were meant to attend to more fundamental questions of truth, beauty, and goodness, not social policy. In our book we want to argue that some policy questions are of the sort that the humanities are best able to deal with. After all, many (perhaps most) policy questions are moral in nature, and it is silly to think we can deal with moral problems without a moral philosophy. Our position is that it is not *a priori* inappropriate for the humanities to be involved in social issues. There are really two questions here: Should the humanities in principle be engaged with social questions? And, secondly, how can they do so effectively? One could agree that the humanities ought to be so engaged, but still hold that they don't do it well or even aren't equipped to do it well because of flaws in the way the humanities are taught or for some other reason.

BM—What is your own view on the relationship between the humanities and public policy?

DC—I start with the assumption that the desire to find a way of relating the humanities and public policy was and is perfectly legitimate. So far as I know, no one has flatly denied the pertinence of the humanities to public policy concerns. It is the nature of that pertinence that is in question. If a fundamental purpose of the humanities is to reflect upon and to attempt to understand the human condition, to explore questions of ends, meanings, interpretations, justifications, past memories, and present purposes, then how can they fail to have something of value for the formation of public policy? If a basic purpose of public policy is finding ways to devise a more just, humane, and sensitive economic and political order, how can that not, in turn, be pertinent to the work of humanities?

BM—Are you suggesting that the humanities are too ivory-towerish?

DC—I believe that those from the humanities with an interest in policy questions must, on occasion, mix it up in the trenches of political life. The purpose of this is not only to gain a bit of credibility for themselves in the eyes of those who work out in the world of politics and policy, but in order better to understand themselves and the limitations and possibilities of their own disciplines. The humanities are about the only academic fields that do not traffic much beyond the academy. They should, on occasion, if only because those in the humanities need to have their own imaginations and disciplinary potentialities stretched. A steady diet of confronting only students, rather than trying themselves to grapple directly with the problems, is likely to leave them intellectually anemic, far more prone to note and comment on the work of their colleagues than to focus on those larger human questions that provide the fundamental motivation behind the humanities in the first place. If it is true that policy analysis and policy-making, but particularly the latter, are in essence oriented toward action and not toward thought or theory, then it is possible to agree that there is a basic difference between the sphere of the humanities and that of policy. In that sense, the critics of attempts to join the fields are correct.

BM—What do you think the humanities can contribute to social policy?

DC—The first contribution is that of the formation of character. The humanities have an important and traditional role to play in helping to form the traits and virtues necessary for citizens to make sound and sensitive judgments. If policy-making is an art, oriented toward action, then, inevitably, character, fundamental sensitivities, basic human decencies will count very heavily. The second, no less important contribution is providing alternative perspectives, frameworks, and vision. It is an inherent hazard of policy analysis and policy-making to neglect the larger schemes and problems of human life in order to solve immediate problems and meet clamorous demands. The humanities, by reminding people of tradition, of ends and purposes, can provide an important and necessary corrective.

BM—The next question is why don't you think the humanities are making those contributions?

DC—I doubt that anything of value can effectively be done by the humanities unless those whose calling it is to work within them form their own character and take seriously just what it is the humanities are all about. The greatest deformation of the humanities has been to turn them into one more set of specialized disciplines, particularly in their aping of the sciences, or by retreating into the pleasure of the humanities, as into exotic crossword puzzles. The first people those in the humanities have to deal with are themselves. They cannot provide insight for others unless they are able to generate it for themselves.

BM—A case of physician heal thyself.

DC—Exactly.

BM—My impression is that there is a dirty-hands syndrome here. Humanists tend overwhelming to be in what Santayana called the genteel tradition and are quite sniffy when it comes to mixing it up, as you put it, in the trenches of social policy.

DC—The worry is that somehow they will sell their souls for the instant relevance of policy issues, or will sell out their methodological souls for the less elegant, less careful ways of policy formation. I suppose that is a hazard. But the greater hazard is that those in the humanities will forget that they are meant to generate wisdom and insight, vision and perspective. And that is what policy most urgently requires.

BM—How does all of this relate to your own education in the humanities? Were you as a student carrying the torch to society? Or were you off in some Elysian paradise of truth and beauty?

DC—During the late fifties and sixties when I was a student,there was little interest in applied humanities, particularly in philosophy. Ethics itself was scarcely taken seriously, let alone the application of normative ethics to social problems. I got interested in philosophy by reading Socrates. When I went to graduate school the message I got was: "Listen kid, that is not what philosophy is all about. We don't go around talking to people. We do serious work in highly technical fields like logic and the philosophy of language." I was strongly urged to mend my ways.

BM—Did you?

DC—I played the game.

BM—Did you find it agreeable?

DC—No, I found it intolerable.

BM—But you stuck with it.

DC—I did, but I was restless through the whole thing. So much so that when I left graduate school I went into journalism.

BM—Was founding the Hastings Center a reaction against your own education?

DC—It was a reaction against a variety of things. First of all, it was a reaction against understanding the intellectual life in strictly disciplinary terms. As an undergraduate, I liked, and I have always liked, interdisciplinary work. Part of the idea of the Center is to be interdisciplinary. The humanities are central but by no means our only interests. The problems we deal with have many dimensions— scientific, historical, legal, moral, religious, and so forth. Another purpose of the Center was to get people working actively in applied issues. The real question behind the book is how do you do this and how do you do it well. The humanities don't furnish good models for what we are trying to do. Another reason for the Center was to try to do things that were difficult or impossible to do in an academic setting.

BM—That may be changing somewhat. Most universities (and

*even most colleges) now have centers of one kind or another which,
much like your own, are mounting interdisciplinary approaches to
complex social problems. But it remains the case that intellectual
progress is measured by technical progress in the disciplines. Someday someone ought to do a study of the consequences for society of
measuring intellectual achievement in this manner. One can scarcely
think of any other society that has done this to the degree we have.
Some large bills for our efforts may be coming due down the line.*

DC—No doubt. It is hard for me to belive that there exists a single
field of study that cannot benefit from other fields.

*BM—Aren't you, to some extent, a victim of the paradigm you
deplore? After all, you rely in your book largely on academics trained
in specialized ways.*

DC—I hadn't thought of it that way. Part of the problem is that
people schooled in the humanities are mostly in the universities. This
is by and large the only place they can find employment. But I think it
can safely be said that the contributors to this book have shown
broad interests not only in other academic fields but in policy issues
as well. I am sure all of them would share my view of the humanities
as being concerned with the ultimate questions of meaning, good and
evil, right and wrong, history, language, and self-understanding.

*BM—Some would object that this is a somewhat parochial view.
After all, social scientists often claim to be engaged in precisely those
questions. History, for example, is very often classed as a social
science.*

DC—I don't want to get hung up on the structure of meaning and
the like. But it remains true in the main that the humanities are much
more congenial to normative approaches to basic questions.

*BM—Even though some humanities studies are technicized to the
point that the normative has virtually disappeared?*

DC—Despite that, it remains the case that, by reason of their
history and their methodologies, the humanities are more oriented
to the normative. I find the main difference between myself as a
philosopher and my social scientist colleagues is that they are more
interested in describing how cultures work or how people interact
with each other, and I find myself saying, "That's all very well, but
is this the way things ought to be?" Most social scientists would be
inclined to say that ought questions are beyond their field. I would
want to claim that the humanities are overtly responsible for non-
empirical truth.

BM—It is too bad that we let quite artificial disiciplinary distinctions set the parameters of dialogue on these matters. Conversation can only go so far before someone waves a red flag interdicting further passage in that direction. The "my-field-your-field" is perhaps too limited.

DC—It is limited. But there is no easy way around these distinctions, if for no other reason than that these disciplines have a long history behind them and the practitioners of them are legitimately set in certain ways of thinking. I constantly get into this conversation in talking about ethics with physicians. They incline to a situational solution for any problem that might arise and find it difficult to think that Aristotle, for example, would have anything to tell them about how to treat a patient today. It's not hard to get people to take ethics seriously. What is hard is to convince them that there is a discipline out there that would be worth their while looking into.

BM—How do you convince them?

DC—My argument is that problems physicians think they are just discovering actually have a history. I make the point that it is not very intelligent to try to think through issues that others have already thought through and about which there is an accumulated body of knowledge.

BM—Of course, many medical problems today are genuinely new.

DC—They are genuinely new in one sense, but most of them relate to old problems. An example of a new question would be something like the allocation of resources for organ transplants. Who is going to pay for all of this? We have never had a question like that before. On the other hand, it is obviously a question of justice, which is a very old question. A question like allocating resources for organ transplants quickly leads us into other questions like individual versus social good, individual rights, the right to life, etc. You are soon into humanities questions, and they are very old humanities questions. The gist of my argument is that while the literature on these subjects may not be directly applicable to a given medical problem, it at least provides an illuminating context for discussing and solving such problems, and therefore physicians ought to be familiar with it.

BM—Have you ever actually convinced any physicians with that argument?

DC—I would claim some modest success. The great triumph is when someone comes to us with a specific problem and asks for advice. Of course, we can't tell him what to do. I can have an opinion on an issue like anyone else, but it is only an opinion. What I can do is indicate ways of thinking through complex problems and point to the history and literature of analagous problems. The golden rule is that if a problem is tough, there is no canned answer.

BM—*What has been your toughest case?*

DC—Probably the Karen Ann Quinlan case. Her parents' attorney came to us for advice about how to argue in court why her respirator should be disconnected. So did the state attorney general and the prosecutor of Morris County, New Jersey. The day after she died we took calls from some 30 different organizations to discuss the ethical issues raised by the Quinlan case.

BM—*One problem might be that medicine tends to be a rather precise science, while ethics is often general if not vague.*

DC—I don't think so. I don't think in this respect ethics is very different from medicine. In clinical practice, there are no two cases the same. A vast and varied network of circumstances surrounds every case, including many nonmedical circumstances. So when physicians ask us for precise answers, we caution them not to expect more precision from us than they are capable of in their own practices. In the end, what is required in both cases is judgment. That is why medicine is an art. No physician has ever devised an answer to what precisely must be done with this patient, suffering from this disease, at this particular point in time. Like anything else, it is often not a question of what answer we come up with but how we understand the problem. And this means, among other things, developing an appropriate language for talking about the problem.

BM—*Why does the Hastings Center focus on problems in medical ethics rather than, say, policy issues? There are lots of problems in the world.*

DC—I suppose it grew out of my own experience. Back in the sixties I got interested in the problem of abortion, which struck me as a problem that called for many different approaches. In fact, it was while trying to work through that problem that I got the idea for the Center as a place where complex issues could be worked on from an interdisciplinary approach. Also, medical questions are unusually interesting because they raise in such fundamental ways questions of good and evil and the nature of man. I make a distinction between natural and artifactual problems. The treatment of dying patients would be a natural ethical issue. This is an ultimate situation where

we have to ask what we mean by life and death. An artifactual
problem is one that is generated primarily by our social arrangements. An example would be how to use data in social science
research. We've looked at ethical problems in other fields, but medicine has more of them than all the others put together, and they are
more interesting. I just came back from a meeting of the American
Medical Association at which the profession was trying to anticipate
some of the problems facing them in the next five years. It is gratifying for me to see that ethics is right there on the agenda along with
questions of medical technology and economics.

BM—*What message do you carry to such conferences?*

DC—I simply point out that there was a time when ethical issues
were thought in the medical profession to be on the fringe, and now
they are central. To be a competent medical practitioner today
involves ethical judgments. This is because the profession, in face of
unprecedented problems, is re-evaluating itself and its role in society.
A good illustration is termination of treatment. There comes a time
when the physician's technical skills are simply irrelevant because the
problem facing him or her is ethical in nature. I am trying to deal with
all of this in a book I am trying to write on medical ethics.

BM—*Tell us about that.*

DC—I've become quite dissatisfied with the standard way of doing
medical ethics. The standard textbook approach is based on what we
might call the agreed-upon paradigm for doing moral philosophy.
According to this paradigm, one solves problems by appealing to
moral rules and principles like autonomy, beneficence, or justice.
These rules and principles are further grounded in some ethical
theory like utilitarianism. That is basically the way all moral philosophy is taught, including bioethics. I must confess I don't find this a
very helpful paradigm.

BM—*What's the matter with it?*

DC—The basic problem with it is that it is too formalistic. Not
only does it not tell us in any helpful way what to do when confronted
with a problem, but it is actually misleading because it allows the
culture to stuff the method with its real content. Suppose you have a
problem with a handicapped infant. Say the problem is whether to
keep it alive or let it die. According to the paradigm, what one is
supposed to do is consult a rule like beneficence which in turn says
that we must act in the best interests of the child. Now for me the
interesting question is: What are the best interests of the child? Or

take the question of euthanasia. For about 20 years now, we have acknowledged as a principle that people ought to be able to choose when they want to die and be in control of their own destiny. Up to a point that's fine. But the real question is: When should I want to die? There are other questions. How much pain ought I be willing to bear? What is my obligation to others? What do I owe to myself? To my body? An ethic of autonomy doesn't give me a clue in answering questions like that. What one ought to do with one's freedom is a question the traditional paradigm has not been able to accommodate. This has been assumed to be beyond the realm of rational discourse or a matter of subjective preference. What the paradigm does is provide the facade or moral rules and principles, but the really hard questions are skirted. Our moral theories talk about maximizing individual freedoms and protecting the best interests of the disadvantaged, but they have no concrete content. Rules and principles give us the illusion of having a morality, but when it gets to the hard questions, they are of no help at all.

BM—*That sounds like what Hannah Arendt said.*

DC—I'm not making the connection. What did she say?

BM—*Morality for her was a matter of thinking without a bannister, that is thinking when there are no hard and fast rules to point the way. Moral judgment is the ability to see the particularity of a situation beyond the general application of rules. She didn't think rules helped very much in the crucial existential situations.*

DC—Didn't she say something like that in her book on the Adolph Eichmann trial?

BM—*Eichmann was for her one of those people who can only act when following rules and orders. He lacked utterly the capacity to discern the moral flavor of a situation. He was morally tone deaf, so to speak.*

DC—I wouldn't mind pursuing this line of thinking.

BM—*But then it might turn out that you would be interviewing me, and that wouldn't be nearly as interesting for our readers. Let's turn to some questions in medical ethics, which is, after all, where you and the Hastings Center principally apply the humanities.*

DC—What kind of questions do you have in mind?

BM—*You have a pro-choice position on abortion. Would you be pro-choice on euthanasia?*

DC—I think of euthanasia as the opposite of abortion in important ways. When I did a book on abortion with my wife (who was pro-life) we used to have a running joke. What she wanted was that abortion be illegal but that no woman would be prosecuted for having one. What I wanted was that abortion be legal but that no woman would ever choose to have one. I think euthanasia ought to remain illegal but that we should punish leniently. If a person believes that, then let him take his chances with the legal system and the moral opinion of his fellow citizens.

BM—Wouldn't that practice lead to a relaxation of the law?

DC—Not necessarily, because, in the first place, people do get punished. I am thinking of a case in Florida where a man shot his wife because she was suffering from cancer. He went to jail, and I think he should have gone to jail, because the case has fuzzy edges. It wasn't really clear that the wife wanted to die, although it was quite clear that she had become a burden to her husband. The law is stiff enough to make people think twice.

BM—Still, the logic of abortion and euthanasia strike many people as very similar.

DC—I think the big difference between abortion and euthanasia is the weight of empirical evidence. When I was researching the abortion book, I became convinced that women are going to have abortions no matter what—in all countries, in all cultures, at all ages. I don't think there is an equal compulsion to commit euthanasia. Furthermore, there is no effective way to make abortion illegal. There is considerable moral doubt in my mind about the status of the fetus, so I can, in good conscience, leave that decision up to individuals. I think the fetus has more value than a lot of pro-choice people believe, but I don't have any decisive arguments. Many pro-life people have a kind of domino theory that holds that if you kill a fetus, you will end up committing all sorts of heinous crimes. But that doesn't happen. There is no solid evidence that legalized abortion breeds disrespect for life. When I was doing the book, I looked at a lot of social systems, and I particularly looked at the correlation between abortion and other forms of violence. There was no correlation at all. Japan, for example, has a high abortion rate but great respect for the elderly. But in South America, where abortion is illegal, people are killing one anther in the streets. In the case of euthanasia, the status of life is much different, and I really worry about the spill-over effects if it were legalized.

BM—But at least public opinion now seems to favor legalizing euthanasia.

DC—Yes, that is true, and it raises the question of whether the long-standing Western tradition that rejects active euthanasia and assisted suicide has the intellectual resources to withstand the growing pressures to legitimate them.

BM—What is the best argument against euthanasia?

DC—The traditional religious argument held that self-determination does not extend to a right to take our own life. God alone has the right to take innocent life. The best philosophical argument, I think, comes from John Stuart Mill, who argued that the one exception to our right to do with our person as we will is the right to sell ourselves in slavery. Mill said that the principle of freedom cannot require that we are free not to be free. It is not freedom to be allowed to alienate freedom. There is a parallel here: To cede to another the right to kill us is to give that person the power to remove our freedom once and for all. The reason even voluntary slavery is wrong is not simply that we ought not, in the name of mercy or freedom, be able to alienate our freedom so fundamentally, but also that no other person should be given so total and decisive a power over our life. That is the most basic threat to, or violation of, the right of self-determination that can be imagined. However strong the motive to do so, that fundamental right cannot be set aside without contradicting its very nature. If I am by right master of my fate, I cannot transfer my right of mastery to another, nor can any other person receive it from me. To ask another to be the agent of my death, moreover, would cease to be simply an expression of my isolated autonomy. It would create a profound relationship between that other person and myself, transcending our individual acts. From the side of the person who killed me, his would be an irrevocable act, one that becomes his act as much as mine. From my side, I would be recruiting an accomplice, asking him to take into his hands a decisive power over me, one that could not be recalled once he had acted. I see no moral basis for so ultimate a transfer of the power of life and death. It is more than the principle of self-determination historically has, or morally should, encompass.

BM—I sense a contradiction between the position you take on euthanasia and the position you took on limited allocation of health care to the elderly in your recent book Setting Limits. *I quote a passage from that book: "Even with relatively ample resources, there will be better ways in the future to spend our money than on indefinitely extending the life of the elderly. That is neither a wise social goal nor one that the aged themselves would want, however compel-*

lingly it will attract them." Sounds like a form of euthanasia to me.
DC—A lot of people have made that objection. But I see the two
positions as very different. My contention is that, properly understood, the distinction between killing and allowing to die is still
perfectly valid for use, both in the euthanasia debate and in the
allocation discussion. The distinction rests on the commonplace
observation that lives can come to an end as the result of (a) the direct
action of another who becomes the cause of death (as in shooting a
person), or as the result of (b) impersonal forces where no human
agent has acted (death by lightning or by disease). The purpose of the
distinction is to separate those deaths directly caused by human
action, and those caused by nonhuman events. It is, as a distinction,
meant to say something about human beings and their relationship
to the world. It attempts to articulate the difference between those
actions for which human beings can rightly be held responsible and
those of which they are innocent. At the heart of the issue is a
distinction between physical causality—the realm of impersonal
events—and moral culpability—the realm of human responsibility.
On the one hand, to bring the life of another to an end by an injection
is to directly kill the other—our action is the physical cause of death.
On the other hand, to allow someone to die from a disease we cannot
cure (and that we did not cause) is to permit the disease to act as the
cause of death.

*BM—One could say, on the one hand, that you present a powerful
argument (as I would be inclined to say) or, on the other, that it
carries so much philosophical baggage that it amounts to little more
than sophistry.*

DC—That may be more a comment on the place of philosophy in
our liberal arts curriculum than on any flaw in my argument. I think
the source of much uneasiness with my argument is that we can be
morally culpable of killing someone (unless we have a moral right to
do so, as in self-defense) and no less culpable for allowing someone to
die (if we have both the possibility and the obligation of keeping that
person alive). Thus there are cases where, morally speaking, it makes
no difference whether we killed or allowed to die; we are equally
responsible morally. In those cases, the lines of physical causality and
moral culpability happen to cross. Yet the fact that they can cross in
some cases in no way shows that they are always, or even usually, one
and the same. We can usually dissect the difference in all but the most
obscure cases. We should not, then, use the ambiguity of

such cases to do away altogether with the distinction between killing and allowing to die. Ambiguity may obscure, but it does not erase the line between the two.

BM—Getting back to the humanities book, do you think you accomplished what you set out to do?

DC—I suppose the question we never adequately got to the bottom of was the question of appropriate standards. Do you use the narrow standards of a discipline or some other standard? I see two approaches to the question of standards. Some policy questions can be translated quite literally into the technical language of a discipline. The joural *Philosophy and Public Affairs* is a good example of that approach. It deals with policy issues, but only professional philosophers can grasp the arguments advanced. The other way is to incorporate some of the language and methods of the policy issues themselves and work out some kind of illuminating marriage with the philosophical or value components of those issues. Here the humanities people have to get into the shoes of other professionals and see things from their point of view. This distinction was brought out beautifully at a meeting we had at the Center some time ago with a group of legislative assistants and academics. The legislative types put forth the view that in Congress what counts most is negotiation and compromise. A philosopher rose to the point and said: "But who ever said that compromise and negotiation are good?" Well, that is a fair question, but out of place in that circumstance. We can't be helpful to legislators by raising fundamental philosophical questions. We have to deal with their constraints and be able to raise philosophical questions within those constraints.

BM—Are you basically interested in getting the humanists to come to some agreement among themselves or in having an interdisciplinary dialogue between humanists and other disciplines?

DC—In the book, we were interested in the humanists gaining a better self-understanding. We were really addressing an internal debate within the humanities and focusing on the question of whether it is appropriate for humanists to deal with policy issues. Most of our contributors took the position that, in the very nature of the case, the humanities are applied over against someone like Bill Bennett, who thinks that, in the very nature of the case, the humanities can't be applied. Interestingly enough, the historical evidence is all on the side of applied humanities. The idea that they can't be applied is not only a very constricted one but also a very recent one, coming primarily from the nineteenth century when the humanities battled the sciences for academic turf. ☐

An Interview with
ROBERT COLES On

The Moral Power of Literature

ROBERT COLES is a child psychiatrist who teaches at Harvard University. He is best known as the author of *Children in Crisis*, a five-volume study of children under stress in modern society, for which he received the Pulitzer Prize in 1973. He is also the author of *The Moral Life of Children* and *The Political Life of Children*. Dr. Coles's studies are not only multi-ethnic, but multinational as well. He has written about the rich and the poor, black and white, Eskimos and Indians, Brazilians and Americans, the children of South Africa and of Northern Ireland. His honors, in addition to the Pulitzer Prize, include the Ralph Waldo Emerson Prize of Phi Beta Kappa, the McAlpin Medal of the National Association for Mental Health, the Holzheimer Award from the American Psychiatric Association, and a MacArthur Foundation award. He is a member of many learned societies and a Fellow of the American Academy of Arts and Sciences. Dr. Coles has lent support to a number of social causes, and he is a popular speaker on the campus circuit.

I was able to interview him late last fall, after one of his campus lectures. We sat before an open fire, drank V-8 juice, and talked well into the night. His lecture that evening had been on the subject of moral development. As was his wont, he removed his jacket, leaned over the podium and proceeded to rivet the packed auditorium "with a story or two." His story was about Ruby Bridges—how he met her, how she influenced him, what he learned about moral development from her. It was the summer of 1958. Coles was a captain in the Air Force, stationed in Biloxi, Mississippi, with a vague assignment to keep Strategic Air Command pilots feeling good mentally. One afternoon in the Gentilly section of New Orleans, he was held up by an unusual traffic jam. Coles got out of his car and walked to the scene of all the commotion. That was when he met Ruby Bridges. By federal order she was the first black child to attend Frantz School. Escorted by marshalls, she had to walk through a mob of white people who were screaming threats and obscenities at her. Hear Coles in his own words: "The whole student body was boycotting the school in protest. Ruby had the whole school building to herself. Can you imagine going to school, in the first grade at the age of six, all by yourself, with a teacher who doesn't want to teach you and has been ordered by the judge to stay on duty and teach lest she lose her retirement benefits? Kafka anticipated this scene. A little girl, a school abandoned, a solitary teacher teaching her, and every day, with patience and determination, people standing in front of the building telling her they are going to kill her and insulting her endlessly."

Coles thought Ruby would be an ideal subject to study the effects of stress on young children. In time, he won her confidence, came to know her, and underwent something akin to a conversion experience. He was amazed by Ruby's serenity, her courage, her faith. She actually prayed for her oppressors. Hear Coles again: "Ruby, with all her handicaps, could pray for people who wanted to kill her, could pray long and hard for them, and tell me three years later, 'You know, I used to think about these people, and I used to ask God how it can be that people can be that way, just over someone like me.' A fundamental moment of moral and existential inquiry by a little girl in elementary school, a black child in the segregated society of the American South in 1958. Will we professors somehow be able to equal that in our work and in our moral development? It is at least a question to start us thinking about these matters."

Coles had made his point with the students about moral development.

BM—You have an M.D. in pediatrics, you are a practicing psychiatrist, you teach literature and moral issues to a wide variety of students, you are an outspoken social critic, an amateur theologian, a sought-after public speaker, and widely published writer, among other things. Will the real Robert Coles please stand up?

RC—I would have to say my first love is teaching. About ten years ago, I importuned the dean at Harvard to let me teach a course on literature and medicine, and I fell in love with teaching through literature.

BM—What do you teach in that course?

RC—Many well-known literary figures were also medical doctors. I teach Anton Chekhov, Walker Percy, and William Carlos Williams. I also use a lot of Flannery O'Connor.

BM—Do you teach any of the mainline medical courses?

RC—No.

BM—A course like the one you teach must be unique.

RC—There are other medical schools that use literature. But it is probably fair to say I was a pioneer in that field.

BM—Do you get good response?

RC—Oh, yes. For example, I use Williams's collection called *Doctors' Stories.* That's been a great joy to teach, and it's a wonderful way to get medical students involved in the personal drama of medicine—the challenges and frustrations, the bitterness and the joy that doctors as people experience. This can only be communicated through stories. They get to the heart of medicine in ways technical and social science texts cannot.

BM—Why is story telling so effective?

RC—Because we are the story-telling creature. We are the creature who is both blessed with and afflicted with language. Our fundamental nature is to speak and to listen and to want to know where we come from, what we are, and where we are going. Through story telling we affirm ourselves as human beings. It's that basic.

BM—Do you confine your teaching to the Medical School?

RC—No. Altogether, I teach in five different schools at Harvard. I teach a course in the law school on Dickens and the law in which I use four novels in which lawyers figure: *Bleak House, Tale of Two Cities, Great Expectations*, and *Little Dorritt*. I also teach a regular undergraduate course. Lately I have developed a course on business and literature for the business school, and from time to time I teach in the Kennedy School of Government. For a while, I even taught a course in the school of education.

BM—How do you get through so many doors?

RC—By infiltration mostly. I come up with ideas and try to persuade deans and departmental chairs to let me try them out. I never wanted to teach social science or psychoanalysis or any of the things I was trained for. I like to teach literature, and that satisfies me.

BM—Do you have a degree in literature?

RC—No.

BM—Who were some mentors that influenced your thinking?

RC—I came to know William Carlos Williams as an undergraduate and wrote my senior thesis on his poem *Paterson*. I love literature, but I don't like what professors and the critics do with it. They seem to make of literature an intellectual exercise. Williams taught me that it is a way of reflecting on personal moral experience, a way of developing the moral imagination.

BM—How would you define the moral imagination?

RC—It is the ability to think creatively about our experience and the ability to respond emotionally as well as intellectually to that experience. Williams said that his writings were aimed at the conscience. He said he was out to unnerve people, to get them worried about what they might be doing, or not doing. "If I can get people wondering about what they are doing in life," Williams said, "whether they are doing good or doing bad and how much of each, then I have done something with my life."

BM—What else did you learn from Williams?

RC—I imbibed some of his faith in story telling. I remember, while in medical school, asking him how some of us going into one or another profession might do the kind of reading that would get our moral imagination going—help us break out of whatever particular moral standstill threatened us. He had no easy answers, but he had great faith in story telling. "Hell," he said, "from the Bible onward, a parable, a talk, a story well told creeps into your chest, turns your stomach, makes your eyes widen up, your ears, too. It's not only the brain we're after." His words sure made a difference in my life. They got me thinking, got me ultimately to try medicine, got me also to work with children, as he did, to train in pediatrics and child psychiatry.

BM—So you see a pretty direct relationship between the moral imagination and literature or story telling?

RC—Yes. Literature raises all the basic moral questions.

BM—*Does it give the answers as well?*

RC—In the only way that moral questions can be answered: by indirection. Kierkegaard talked about moral edification. By that he meant that we learn (and teach) morality in all kinds of subtle ways—by example, story telling, irony, humor, innuendo, a whole range of indirections.

BM—*Tell us about the course for the business school.*

RC—That one is called The Business World: Moral and Social Inquiry Through Fiction. We read some of the same authors I use in the medical school. Percy, for example, wrote about a young stockbroker in *The Moviegoer*, and Williams's *Paterson* is about the old factory towns of the Northeast. Williams also wrote a trilogy of novels on the same theme, and they strike at the moral imagination in powerful ways. Flannery O'Connor has a little jewel of a story called "The Displaced Person" about a businesswoman who decides to let an inefficient worker go. This gives O'Connor an opportunity to write about the human passions of greed, selfishness, and hatred. Saul Bellow's *Seize the Day* is good, too. And some of John Cheever's stories about the emptiness of material success. But the best of all, and I start with it, is Scott Fitzgerald's *The Great Gatsby*. Students can make connections between Gatsby and Ivan Boesky and things that are going on in the contemporary business world. I am now in my third year with that course, and I have a great time with it. I am impressed with the seriousness of the students I teach. I receive some very thoughtful letters from them once they get out in the business world.

BM—*And the Kennedy School?*

RC—There I do a seminar that concentrates on one book— Robert Penn Warren's *All the King's Men*. We read the novel, see the movie, plus a documentary on the life of Huey Long. That is ample material for one semester.

BM—*What emerges as the central moral category in the various readings you do?*

RC—In my work with children, I learned that a lot of their moral reflection turns on the idea of responsibility. That seems to be true in literature as well. Responsibility is about loyalty and commitment, about reaching out to others and sharing their burdens, about standing up in dissent. It is easy to let what the Bible calls "principalities and powers" become the exclusive custodians of the meaning of responsibility. But there are times when we have to stand alone no matter what the political or social or even legal hazards.

BM—The biblical idea of sacrificial love seems to be high on your list of virtues.

RC—It is. It is indeed. And that, of course, is not unrelated to responsibility.

BM—When do you do your writing?

RC—In the morning, early.

BM—And your research?

RC—On the three days I don't teach. And, of course, during vacations and sabbaticals.

BM—You must be a workaholic.

RC—No question about it.

BM—Do you work at home?

RC—Yes.

BM—Is your family grown?

RC—I have three boys. One is in medical school. One is a senior in college, and the third is a senior in high school. My wife is a high school English teacher and incidentally the daughter of a Harvard Business School alumnus.

BM—How do you work in your public lectures?

RC—I have to be very careful about that. I do outside lecturing mostly during the nonacademic year. I have never gone on what they call the lecture tour. I do one at a time when I can. And I restrict my lectures to colleges and universities. I don't like speaking to large public audiences. I enjoy students. I don't get drained by them. On the contrary, they nourish me.

BM—What are your political commitments?

RC—I do no political stuff at all.

BM—Weren't you once a political activist?

RC—The last time I was involved in politics was when I worked for Bobby Kennedy. When he died, that was the end for me. Look at what we have had for the last 20 years.

BM—Make a statement about that.

RC—I think Sirhan Sirhan is a major figure in American history. Because of him we have had four presidents—Richard Nixon, Gerald Ford, Jimmy Carter, and Ronald Reagan—we would not otherwise have had, and, as far as I am concerned, should not have had.

BM—What did you like about Bobby Kennedy?

RC—For one thing, his ability toward the end of his life to pull

together the black and white people of this country. What I most
liked about him was his passionate idealism. In fact, that was new to
him. I don't think I would have liked Kennedy ten years earlier. But
towards the end of his life, there was something almost magical about
him, as though a moment of grace had touched American political
life. Since his death, political idealism has virtually disappeared. And
that is very sad. When I was in medical school, I was very taken with
the novels and stories of Salinger. He had a genius for evoking
idealism in his characters, a sense of searching and moral hunger. I
don't see much of that anymore, even in literature.

*BM—A point worth pondering. But you raise a serious question
about citizenship. Can we afford to abandon the political arena?*

RC—I hope not.

BM—Can you afford it?

RC—I've written a book about the political life of children and
investigated at some length how children come by their political
values. I guess what I have done is taken the energies I put into the
civil rights and antipoverty movements and transferred them to my
writing. But, yes, I worry about this. I ask myself if I shouldn't spend
more time struggling on behalf of political and social causes, at least
some of the time rather than none of the time. Shouldn't I be writing
more about these larger issues rather than cultivating my own rather
narrow academic path?

*BM—No one would ever call your path narrow. You are, in fact,
exemplary. Do you encourage your students to become politically
involved?*

RC—I do. In the undergraduate course I teach on literature and
social reflection, I ask my students to do volunteer work like tutoring
and visiting prisons and becoming big brothers and sisters. And I ask
them to write papers about their experiences. This strategy not only
involves them in a form of community action but it also enables them
to make the connection between intellect and conduct. This is so very
important, and it is much neglected. This is the great gap in education
that Ralph Waldo Emerson called attention to a hundred and fifty
years ago in his famous essay "The American Scholar." Character
is higher than intellect, he said. Williams explored that theme as well,
I tell students to read novels because they suggest various
moral, social, and psychological possibilities and stimulate the
mind's capacity to wonder, to dream, to put itself in all sorts of
situations, and to be shaped by such imaginative experiences.

But that isn't enough. They also have to go and do. They have to become participants not only in their own experience but in the life of their communities. This is the existential crux of education. We have to be as well as know. And this doesn't mean becoming an anti-intellectual. We can learn from books. There we learn about human experience—in James Agee, Orwell, and Chekhov. That isn't the same thing as having those experiences. But once having gained some experience, students can go back to those books and have their own experience illuminated. I don't have any problems beginning with books so long as the experience follows. And, of course, so long as the students go back to the books.

BM—Doesn't the split between intellect and conduct run like a yellow stripe down the spine of the whole educational system?

RC—It's an unfortunate form of segregation, as bad as racial segregation. Maybe the Supreme Court should rule it illegal.

BM—What can we do about it?

RC—I've been explaining what I am trying to do. I am trying to teach literature as serious moral texts.

BM—Is there any one book that has influenced you more than any other?

RC—Perhaps *Anna Karenina*. I read it early in life, and I reread it often. It has become an important part of my personal life. To go back to that novel and try to come to terms with what Tolstoy was trying to come to terms with in light of my own experience is a robust exercise in moral self-awareness. A man like Tolstoy knew more psychology than the whole twentieth-century social science scene will ever know. All this stuff about the stages of dying coming out now—why not just go back and read *The Death of Ivan Ilyich*? It said everything. And who has added any wisdom to the field of marital problems since *Anna Karenina*? I simply wander around from one place to the next, teaching these novels and trying to, in a way, undo the devil in the medical school, law school, and business school. I've also discovered Tolstoy's powerful story "Master and Man." It's about a rich Russian businessman and his servant. The gist of the story is that, while they are on a long trip, they are overtaken by a blizzard, and the businessman, who has never given any attention to anything besides making money, undergoes a moral transformation and saves the life of his poor servant. When I ask my students to read stories like that I hope there will be a moral engagement that will have an ongoing effect on their lives, as it has had on my own.

BM—And you think that happens?

RC—Yes.

BM—What is your evidence?

RC—I'll give you an example. One of my students had taken two courses in moral reasoning at Harvard. He read Walker Percy's *The Second Coming* and came across the line, "You can get all A's in school and flunk life." Afterwards he came to see me and said, "You know, I am beginning to realize that although I got two A's in moral reasoning, I may be flunking life." I asked him why he thought that. He said, "Because in my private life I behave like a first class skunk." I told him that was the most important thing he had learned in college. He had come to an insight that could transform his life. We had a long discussion about how treacherous intellectual life can be when it is segregated from conduct.

BM—Do you get enough of that kind of feedback to satisfy you as a teacher?

RC—You can get it if you want it, if you are willing to take the risk.

BM—Do you have a favorite quote?

RC—I like this one from Agee: "All that each person is, and experiences, and shall ever experience, in body and mind, all these things are differing expressions of himself and of one root, and are identical: and not one of these things nor one of these persons is ever quite to be duplicated, nor replaced, nor has it ever quite had precedent: but each is a new and incommunicably tender life, wounded in every breath and almost as hardly killed as easily wounded: sustaining, for a while, without defense, the enormous assaults of the universe."

BM—As we talk, there are two books about higher education that are riding high in best sellerdom: Allan Bloom's The Closing of the American Mind *and E.D. Hirsch's* Cultural Literacy. *What do you think about them?*

RC—What troubles me about the Hirsch book is that it is yet another list. Americans love lists. I read the book and said to myself: That's interesting. I wish everyone would read the list. They are good books. Cultural literacy is a good thing. But something is missing. What we need is moral literacy. The question we have to ask is: Suppose we read all of the books on Hirsch's list? What then? What use are we going to put this knowledge to? We don't ask that question. Why don't we? Another thing about the list approach is that it seems to assume there was a point in the past when we had a more ideal situation. I don't read history that way. Look at this country fifty years ago. We had vicious race riots, lynchings, segregation. At Harvard at the beginning of this century, there was a lot of cultural literacy but blacks couldn't live in dorms, women weren't admitted, and there were strict quotas on Catholics and Jews. This nostalgia is very historical, and in Bloom's book it reaches a pitch of meanness about contemporary life and about students in particular that I find very distasteful. I ask myself: Why are these books so influential? What do they tell us about ourselves now? I have the impression these authors aren't connected to students, to an ongoing dialogue with young people. When I read Bloom's book, I don't recognize the young people I teach. He is afflicted with a kind of Tory smugness that is very unattractive. What he is saying is that some of us are quite wonderful and enlightened and always have been, and the rest of us are, to use the scientific term, *merde.*

BM—You have spent much of your life with the poor and disadvantaged and written movingly about them. What are your observations about the affluent, middle-class students most of us teach and who, in fact, you teach at Harvard?

RC—Well, I wrote about them in the last volume of my *Children in Crisis* series. It was called *Privileged Ones: The Well-off and the Rich in America.* I think that is my best book, but the reviewers weren't too excited about it. There I talked about one of the great ironies of life: Among the poor, we expect to find defeat and despair, and I found some, to be sure, but I also found strength and hope and courage. Among the rich, we expect to find fulfillment and happiness, and I found some, to be sure, but I found also much boredom, alienation, and decadence. I also found that the rich are apt to have a more diminished sense of compassion. Like the elder brother in *The Brothers Karamozov*, they tend to love humanity in general but less likely to love one person in particular.

BM—Still, don't we more or less assume that the affluent, middle-class way of life is the norm of America?

RC—We do. And we should think searchingly about that. It is ironical that humanitarians work all their lives to improve the condition of the lower classes so that they, too, can experience the despair of boredom.

BM—Doesn't this tend to a romantic view of poverty? After all, we know a lot of homelessness and drug abuse and children born out of wedlock. Doesn't it all add up to a pretty sad picture?

RC—It does. I don't want to be romantic. I don't want to glorify poverty, and I don't want to glorify wealth. What I want to do is try to locate the moral fulcrum in human nature, and I find that what matters most in men and women lies entirely apart from wealth. I have known human beings who, in face of unbearable daily stress, respond with resilience, even nobility. And I have known others who live in a comfortable, even luxurious, environment and yet seem utterly lost. We have both sides in all of us all the time. Some reviewers criticize me for saying the same old things about the nature of human beings: that we are a mixture of good and evil, of light and darkness, of potentiality toward destruction and redemption. They want some new theory, I suppose. But my research merely confirms what the Bible said long ago about human nature and what the world's great literature confirms as well.

BM—How do you account for the springs of your own motiva- tion? What makes you the way you are?

RC—A series of accidents, I guess. When I graduated from col- lege, I never thought I would be a teacher. I never thought I would ever go back to Harvard.

BM—Was your undergraduate experience a good one?

RC—Yes. Perry Miller, the authority on early American Puritan- ism, was one of my mentors, and I have already mentioned the influence of William Carlos Williams. After college, I joined the Air Force and was sent to Mississippi where I was put in charge of a military psychiatric hospital. I fought to go to England or Japan or any other country where we had bases. Mississippi seemed like the worst assignment in the world. Yet it turned out to be a redemptive experience and really changed my life because it was in the South in the sixties that I became involved in the civil rights movement. I stayed there eight years after I got out of the service and began my *Children in Crisis* series during that time. I came back to Harvard because Erik Erickson was teaching there, and I wanted to study with him. He was getting on in years but still very vital and still the best analyst I knew. He made more sense than anyone else. I became one of his teaching assistants and it was then, in my mid-thirties, that I discov- ered that I loved teaching. Erikson told me it was the most nourishing thing I could do. So I see my life as a series of accidental moments. If I were to give myself any credit, I suppose I could say that I was able to seize those moments and turn them into occasions of per- sonal commitment. Also, there was a kind of cranky rebelliousness driving me. I was fed up with social science talk and the jargon of psychiatry. I wondered how people could use their minds this way. I have always moved back and forth from one discipline to another out of a personal struggle to find myself. As a student, I went to work in Dorothy Day's Catholic Worker soup kitchen in Lower Manhattan just to get away from the medical school and get my mind off memorizing lists and do something that made more personal sense.

BM—Did you come from a religious family?

RC—My mother was religious. She was an Episcopalian, and my father was Jewish, but not religious.

BM—Is that an important part of what drives you?

RC—It was. But I let it go in medical school and came back to it during the civil rights movement. In those black churches in the rural South, I began to realize how much religion meant, and how religion could be a mighty force for social reform. As a result of that, my own religion came back to me.

BM—In one of your books, you describe yourself as an agnostic.

RC—That must have been one of the earlier ones. Of course, I still think of myself as a kind of agnostic. Religious faith is accompanied by a lot of doubt. A lot of doubt. Now that I am in my fifties, I find myself interested in how children develop their religious beliefs. I spend time asking them what they learn in Sunday school, what the Bible means to them, how they understand God.

BM—How important is religion?

RC—Nothing I have discovered about the makeup of human beings contradicts in any way what I learn from the Hebrew prophets such as Isaiah, Jeremiah, and Amos, and from the Book of Ecclesiastes, and from Jesus and the lives of those he touched. Anything that I can say as a result of my research into human behavior is a mere footnote to those lives in the Old and New Testaments.

BM—Does psychiatry provide helpful insights into social reality?

RC—Sometimes. At its best, it is a contemporary expression of the I-Thou tradition.

BM—That wasn't what Freud had in mind.

RC—No, but some of it ended up that way. Freud wanted psychiatry to be a science. But there is a religious side to it which he fought hard to keep out but which is there nonetheless, and it is very important.

BM—Didn't Freud also say that when you begin to ask about the meaning of life you are already sick?

RC—He did. But he was wrong about that.

BM—Do you still practice psychiatry?

RC—I still see a few patients.

BM—Children?

RC—I work with children in my research, but I take mostly college and medical students on a very selective basis. The danger is when you see person after person, hour after hour. That becomes draining. You become an automaton. That is why I never had a private practice as such. I see patients on an individual basis, and I don't take money. I like that kind of doctoring. I think I am worried about what Gabriel Marcel called a psychiatric fact man.

BM—Looking through that particular lens, how would you measure the psychic health of our society?

RC—I agree with a lot of what Christopher Lasch said in *The Culture of Narcissism*. Unfortunately, much psychiatry has become a part of that very narcissism. There is a lot of what George Eliot in *Middlemarch* called unreflecting egoism. With the help of psychoanalysis, that often becomes reflecting egoism, which isn't any better. There is not enough reaching out; there is not enough struggle to become a self in the Augustinian sense. I wish we were as interested in moral responsibility as we are in psychological insight.

BM—What difference would that make?

RC—I think it would make us better indeed. If psychoanalysis can't transform us as persons, then it isn't helpful.

BM—Can it?

RC—At its best it can.

BM—Can education?

RC—I think they both can. And do you know what it comes down to? The particular student and the particular teacher, the particular patient and the particular doctor. In other words, the I-Thou relationship.

BM—Americans are often said to be a religious people. One would think that they are to that extent a less selfish people.

RC—Not necessarily, because there is the religion of the letter and the religion of the spirit. Americans are more often interested in the former.

BM—Who, in the final analysis, is responsible for the moral fiber of our society?

RC—We all are. We are all responsible for what this country is because it is our country. And we are all responsible for what this

world is because it is our world. We can't get off the hook by pointing
a finger at some institution when things go wrong.
   BM—You are best known for your Children in Crisis *series. It now
seems to be the case in this country that a certain percentage of our
youth are systematically excluded from the educational system and
predestined to become part of a permanent underclass. What are
your thoughts about how these children can best be helped?*
   RC—I don't know the answer to that. But I know one thing: We
have to reach out. Let me tell you a story about my son, who is a high
school senior. He spent last summer working with a group called
Compass. They work in the greater Boston area with the most
disadvantaged children. He learned a lot from that experience. The
idea that comes to me is that in this country there are thousands and
thousands of college students who could be mobilized to help these
children. We send them to Paris and Spain to learn languages, and
we have internships galore. Why not something like a domestic peace
corps for the underprivileged? Most communities in this country
have at least one college. If the resources of that college were tapped
and properly organized to reach out to these children at the local
level, we would have taken a giant step toward solving the problem,
as well as a number of other social problems. Harvard just got a gift
for 50 million dollars for business ethics. I asked my class at the end
of last semester how they thought that money should be spent. They
said we should go into the ghettos and teach the kids there and inspire
them to find a place in the mainstream, and that, in the long run, will
help us all.
   *BM—Isn't it the case that more students are engaging in this kind
of extracurricular activity?*
   RC—Yes, but don't call it extracurricular. That demeans it. I have
heard many students sharply, and properly, challenge such use of the
phrase "extracurricular." They object to this false distinction between their intellectual life and their work in, say, a ghetto neighborhood. After all, isn't the mind kept busy in many important ways
when one leaves a campus to work in a neighborhood where people
live constantly in great jeopardy? When a student crosses the ocean
to study French or Spanish for a year, or to assist in a social scientist's
"field work," we have no reluctance to consider such an effort intellectual and worthy of academic credit. But when that same student
spends time working with people who, after all, live in a world as
different in certain respects as some of those studied by

anthropologists and sociologists, they are pursuing an "extracurricular" acitivity. Is this the right way to respond to the substantial amount of personal commitment involved in tutoring needy children, feeding the homeless in soup kitchens, and reaching out to vulnerable families to provide medical or legal assistance? When I listen to my students describe what they see and hear in voluntary "extracurricular" activities, I realize how much they are learning. Surely, we who teach in universities can develop courses that will respond to the challenge of student voluntarism—that connect its moral energy with the life of the mind.

BM—Campus Compact is an organization that has been recently formed that might do something like what you are asking.

RC—It's a healthy sign. The question I ask myself is: Why can't we do this? It doesn't take an act of Congress, or a grant, or large scale social studies. It is relatively simple to identify problems at the local level, and I don't think it takes a high degree of creativity to organize our students in some such way as I have suggested. And it isn't just a matter of *noblesse oblige*. We are, as my students pointed out, helping ourselves in the long run. And, furthermore, we have a lot to learn. It isn't as though we were high-minded missionaries going to the natives. Last summer, my son learned important things about sociology, psychology, urban problems, and other things as well. I look upon such activity as educational in the highest sense of the word.   □

An Interview with
EDWIN DORN on
Racism in America

ED DORN is an astute commentor on questions of race, one of the best in the country. This interview originated on a sunny afternoon in Annapolis, Maryland, and continued for several hours later on in Dorn's office at the Joint Center for Political Studies in Washington. It was just after the bicentennial of the Constitution, and Dorn began by making the point that blacks were clearly at a disadvantage when the Republic was established. "Race matters in the United States," he said, "because the nation's founders agreed that it would matter. The Constitution established a national policy of racial inequality. Article V served to perpetuate the slave trade. Article IV guaranteed that fugitive slaves would be returned to their owners. Article I established that slaves would count as three-fifths of a person for purposes of allocating Congressional seats and taxes among the several states. The implication that blacks were to be considered partial people had profound and lasting effects."

Great progress has been made, of course, in the intervening two centuries. We eliminated slavery, established the right of suffrage for blacks, and launched civil rights programs. Dorn pointed out a number of anomalies about our progress toward racial equality. For one thing, it always takes a wrenching and dramatic experience to take the first steps. The Civil War and the civil rights movement of the 1960s hardly fell within the parameters of business as usual. But each time a significant event took place, various forces conspired to arrest change before fundamental racial injustices could be corrected. I asked him to elaborate. He singled out three. One, he said, is the innate conservatism of the constitutional system. Another is the racial conservatism of the white population, the white determination to resist changes that threaten their supremacy over blacks. A third is the tendency of political leaders to destroy the purposes of the original changes. I asked Dorn for an example of the latter. He cited the *Slaughterhouse* decision by Justice Miller in 1873, which declared that the "one prevading purpose" of the Civil War Amendments was to establish the equality of the races in all respects. But, said Dorn, by the 1990s that one prevading purpose was all but forgotten. "The steps needed to convert blacks to whole, free citizens were not taken." Another clear example, he went on, "was the Civil Rights Act of 1964. That was a notable achievement. But that legislation was curiously diverted in the ensuing years with the result that our efforts at racial equality have become very confused."

It was at this point that I turned on my tape recorder.

BM—How do you see the problem of racism in America?

ED—I see it as a tangle of confusions. We have gone through a civil rights movement, which really lasted some 200 years, during which we talked about two things. We talked about equal rights for individuals, and we talked equal rights for races—that is groups of people. The question we have to ask is, How are our efforts to promote political equality and individual rights related to racial equality? And the answer is, The two may not be related at all. We have confused the race issue with the class issue.

BM—What caused us to do that?

ED—At the time Lyndon Johnson was promoting his social programs, there were many more poor folks than there were black folks. And indeed there still are. So inevitably the tendency was to class-based solutions.

BM—I guess that distinction is not clear in my mind. If both blacks and whites share certain problems like poverty, why wouldn't they benefit by common solutions? If you solve some of the class problems, wouldn't you solve at least some of the racial problems?

ED—You do to the extent that blacks are exceptionally poor, and that is why the civil rights approach made sense. But let's for the sake of argument look at the problem in a rarefied conceptual form. I can imagine a society in which the economic gap between the poorest individuals and the richest individuals is much smaller than it is today. I can imagine a society, for example, in which, as a result of support programs, no family has less than an income of ten thousand dollars a year, and the richest would not make more than a million. That would be greatly collapsed income distribution in this country. But it is still possible in that greatly collapsed distribution that blacks would still be at the bottom and whites still at the top. In other words, we would still have racial inequality. I can also imagine a society in which an average median income for blacks is approximately the same as it is for whites. But that could be a society in which the gap between the poorest and the richest is even greater than it is today. That could be a society in which there are reduced racial inequalities but exaggerated class inequalities. We have to understand that choice. And I don't think we have posed it very clearly to ourselves.

BM—How can we pose it more sharply?

ED—By drawing more clearly the distinction between rights and opportunities on the one hand and results on the other. Equal opportunity means a black and a white might wind up in very different positions. If that is true for individuals, might it not also be true for groups? And if that is true, might we not be engaged in a monumental farce when we talk about racial equality?

BM—Are you implying that the civil rights movement failed?

ED—It didn't fail so much as not finish the job. It didn't address the question of equality between groups of people. Nor did it address the question of economic equality.

BM—So what follows from that?

ED—What follows from that is that we are greatly confused over what we are about as a society, and we produce legislation which has confusing and conflicting purposes.

BM—Such as?

ED—The 1960s war on poverty is a good example. We began with the civil rights movement, and then Lyndon Johnson moved on to the war on poverty and the Great Society. Many of us who supported both saw them as closely related. Johnson said as much in his famous "shackled runner" speech at Howard University, in which he said, in effect, we have done all this stuff to deal with rights, but it is difficult for people to take advantage of those rights if they have been historically disadvantaged. Now that we have equalized rights, we need to move to give people equal potential to use their rights. That seemed at the time to be a logical extension of the civil rights movement. Blacks and liberal whites supported it because the agenda seemed to have a racial objective. But we remember Johnson's genius was to broaden coalitions. Soon after the Howard University speech, he showed up in Harlem County, Kentucky, with the message that the war on poverty was for everybody, including the poor whites in Appalachia. It was political sense. It also made a good deal of moral sense because whether you are a white in Harlem County, Kentucky, or a black in Harlem, New York, if you are poor, you are disadvantaged. That is self-evident. But the problem with that approach is that we put a racial objective and a class objective together with the result that we confused the two. And we have been wrestling with that problem ever since. That confusion has greatly perverted our political discourse in the past decade or so.

BM—Give me an example of how political discourse has been perverted.

ED—You often hear people say: We have had all these civil rights measures, and there are still poor black folks, so obviously, civil rights didn't ease black poverty. Others say: We heap all this money on people as a result of the war on poverty, yet there is still an economic gap between blacks and whites. Then the conclusion is drawn that the civil rights movement failed because it didn't solve the poverty problem. The Great Society failed because there are still massive inequalities in our society. What we have to acknowledge to ourselves, if we are honest, is that one purpose was being served by the civil rights legislation, including its later iterations of affirmative action and all that, and a quite different purpose was being served by all the programs associated with the war on poverty. The two would yield very different results.

BM—But neither one cured the problems it was designed to do.

ED—That is true, and it is due largely to the contradiction I mentioned. Of course, there were other reasons. One of them was that our interest flagged. Johnson left office in 1968. Nixon retained the programs but with much less vigor for another two or three years. Then during the seventies, there was greater retrenchment. The money has grown, but imagination and energy have not. And I should say, too, the war on poverty programs flagged more than the civil rights programs. The latter showed a more dynamic curve as other groups like women, Hispanics, the elderly, and the handicapped began to see in the black movement the key to their own problems. But by broadening the base, we also confused the purpose and further dissipated energies. And that is a fundamental political dilemma we still live with.

BM—What purpose was confused?

ED—What we had in mind in the civil rights movement was merely to extend rights to a group who had hithertofore been denied them. We have had in mind that by extending rights we would also achieve some substantive results. In his *American Dilemma*, published in 1944, Gunnar Myrdal tried to explore the relationship between the denial of rights and poverty, on the assumption that there was a relationship. He began by studying poverty in the South and kind of backed into the civil rights question. He said that the reason blacks were poor was because they were denied basic rights and further reasoned that if we can provide rights, we can kill two birds with one stone. America could resolve its 200-year-old dilemma over rights and, by rights, also resolve many of the economic inequalities between the races. Unfortunately, Myrdal didn't get it right.

BM—Where did he go wrong?

ED—From statements about rights, nothing follows about results. Myrdal committed the fallacy, as much of our legislation has, of thinking that something does follow. And, it is also true that from statements about individual rights, nothing follows about results for groups.

BM—Would the opposite be true? In socialist economies it would seem that when group interests are satisfied, then individual interests also are.

ED—Yes. In America we focus on individual rights and we recognize that will often lead to egregious economic inequalities. We see them as a natural result of the different capacities people have to exercise their rights. That's the classical liberal view. Socialists, the Soviets for example, emphasize substantive results. But to get that, they have to deny individual rights and enforce equality. That is a form of political repression.

BM—Which you would not accept?

ED—Which I would not accept. Obviously we need a philosophy that accommodates the two extremes in some middle ground. And there is actually an important debate going on in this country right now about redefining democracy to promote some of the substantive ends I suggest.

BM—Is the right to vote a substantive right?

ED—No, because nothing follows from it. It only means I have the right to vote. It doesn't mean I will actually vote.

BM—What about the right to education?

ED—Well, that depends. We have been arguing about that for a long time. Do we mean every kid ought to have an opportunity to go to school? Do we mean that every kid ought to go to basically the same kind of school? (That would imply equalizing resources.) Do we mean every kid ought to learn the same thing, that is, equality of educational attainment? If we are striving for equal results we have at some point to impose unequal treatment. When we have different starting points, we have to do something to equalize them. That concern has motivated various compensatory education programs. Head Start would be a good example and a direct outcome of LBJ's "shackled runner" speech.

BM—How well are these programs working?

ED—Not as well as they could for a couple of reasons. One, we never put enough money into these programs to adequately compensate for the gaps. More importantly, and we discovered this much later on, the gap in achievement actually grows over time. Kids are more equal in the first grade than they are in the twelfth. There is an easy answer for this, and it is basically the environmental answer. Normally, we assume a kind of stair-step progression through the grades. But for some kids, that doesn't happen because some environments actually make kids forget what they learned and, even worse, motivate them not to learn. Their environments lack the kinds of necessary support systems. This leads quite naturally to the question, What are we going to do about end results? As I pointed out, what we wanted from the civil rights movement was not just opportunity. We wanted a lot more blacks to graduate from high school, to go to college, to enter professional life. That is not happening as we had hoped.

BM—What would be involved in putting more emphasis on results?

ED—More money, obviously. We haven't been willing to do that. Why? Because that contradicts a very strict interpretation of equal rights. We are perceived as giving more to some than to others. Our reforms so far have been the necessary, but not the sufficient, condition for attaining racial equality. Now, of course, logically the necessary has to precede the sufficient. It made political sense to concentrate on rights in the beginning and not front-load the agenda with too much economic talk. Johnson saw what the next step had to be. He saw the sufficient condition question. But the country got bogged down and eventually was exhausted by the traumatic events of the late sixties, especially the Vietnam War.

BM—Is economic equality the sufficient condition we seek?

ED—Not entirely. We have first to talk about conditions necessary to achieve economic equality. But that is the goal.

BM—Why didn't people talk about economic equality as the real goal of the civil rights movement in the beginning?

ED—I think the reason is because people involved in the civil rights movement were afraid of being branded communists. Remember, we were just emerging from the era of McCarthyism, and J. Edgar Hoover and others tried very hard to label Martin Luther King a communist. Hoover went to extraordinary lengths to connect the civil rights movement with some communist conspiracy. So it was very prudent of King and others not to play into Hoover's hands by using expressions like economic equality.

BM—Or any other expression with the word economic in it.

ED—Right. So the language had to be very broad. The strategy was to move rights into the mainstream. Now we have to go back and explain why economic advantages did not flow from the rights premise.

BM—What is the missing piece in the puzzle now?

ED—The real economic gap between blacks and whites has not closed appreciably in the last 30 years. The black median income is still about 55 percent of the white median income. There have been ups and downs over the past 30 years. For example, things looked good in the early 1970s when the ratio was 61 or 62 percent. Since then, things have not gotten any better, and by some measures they have gotten worse. Everybody is better off, but the ratio hasn't changed.

BM—The black family structure has changed for one thing.

ED—That is part of the difference. Also, the structure of the inner city, where most blacks live, has changed in terms of economics and job opportunities.

BM—What kind of question do you ask now? In other words, where do you pick up the sufficient condition question?

ED—It seems to me we have had the answers for a long time. We just haven't been willing to act on them. If we are to rectify racial inequalities, we have to have racial remedies as opposed to class remedies. I have no objection to class remedies. They are much needed. But we have to bear in mind that they are very different from racial remedies. The Supreme Court has said time and again that if you have a racial problem you have to have a racial remedy.

BM—What is a racial remedy?

ED—Examples would be improved compensatory educational programs. Black kids still don't get the same start in life. Also, strongly enforced affirmative action programs in college admissions up front and in employment at the back. I would add more job training programs and subsidized child care for working mothers.

BM—I did an interview with Barbara Jordan some time ago in which she told me, "What we as black people are finding is that we have to dig deeper inside ourselves, to see whether or not we have the resources to deal with problems that seem to be endemic to black people in this country." What I took her to mean was that ultimately there are no policy solutions to the problems of blacks. Ultimately it is a matter of will, moral resolve, or attitudinal changes if you will.

ED—That is surely necessary. We have to change attitudes and incentives. Take a black kid in the inner city who can make several hundred a day peddling crack. Why should he go to school? We have to overcome a great deal of cynicism in the inner city which says that even with a good education you are not going to get a decent break.

BM—Someone has said that generating the political will to solve a problem is nine-tenths of the solution.

ED—We can argue about fractions, but you identify an important component. Political will means understanding the issues, it means leadership, it means motivation, it means the art of politics—forming the necessary coalitions, tapping the financial and institutional resources, organizational skills, community talent, and so forth. A moral effort must accompany policy measures. But bear in mind that we cannot separate the two components too sharply. Head Start, for example, is a policy. But as a program it packs moral clout. In Head Start, students learn values, become motivated, change attitudes, and so forth. I would make a distinction between political will and moral will. Political will is policy; moral will is something like individual efficacy. But, again, the one influences the other. Political will generates moral will. The Great Society offers an example. The federal government then supported many grass-roots programs that produced leaders, got people involved, gave them a great sense of control over their lives. George Will said the Voting Rights Act wouldn't keep black teenage girls from getting pregnant. To which one can only say: Yes, George, that is true. Nor will the Voting Rights Act prevent you from noticing the obvious. A Voting Rights Act is to help people vote, but such measures also empower people.

BM—Could we now say that the sufficent condition formula would include policy measures (that is, government initiatives) and moral will (that is, individual resolve)?

ED—I would add that we have to face up to our problems more honestly. We have shoved a lot of them into the closet because they are too embarrassing or whatever. The black family is a case in point. Senator Daniel Moynihan called attention to the problems of the black family in his famous report of 25 years ago. That is something to worry about. Because the continuing deterioration of the family will greatly compromise the effect of programs. And it has to be said that the black family problem has grown worse since Moynihan's report. The conservative critique is on target here.

BM—Speaking of conservative, is there a conservative intelligentsia among blacks?

ED—There is a small group of successful black intellectuals who have become successful by pretending that race is not important. That's ironic. If race is not important, how can they make so much money saying it isn't important? This group holds two positions I disagree with: One, they advocate race-neutral policies, and, two, they claim that the beneficiaries of affirmative action programs are largely the middle class blacks who would have done well anyway. Think of how the police and fire departments were integrated. No one has yet demonstrated to me that a black policeman in Memphis or Cleveland was middle class before he got that job. This group also tends to emphasize negative rights while I am advocating positive rights.

BM—Does that make you a liberal?

ED—I'm chary of labels like that. Reagan was supposed to be a conservative, and two things conservatives stand for are fiscal restraint and limited government. Reagan wasn't a conservative in either of those senses. So I try to think through problems without benefit of labels.

BM—How do you assess black leadership at this point in time?

ED—We don't have any Kings. But that has to be a good thing because at this stage we don't need one. Partly as a result of King's own influence, there are now thousands of black leaders. At the time of the March on Washington, you could put all the black leaders in one room. Now it would take a convention hall or two. Also, the leadership is more broadly based. Traditionally, black leadership came from the ministers because they were the only ones who couldn't be fired by the white folks. This is all to the good, but it brings some disadvantages because it leads to a diffusion of energies and purposes. Whereas, formerly, black leaders came together around a few central problems, we now tend to argue a lot about many problems.

BM—You can probably live with that. Someone predicted that the central problem in America in the twentieth century would be the color line. That seems to have largely come true. Do you think that will be the case for the twenty-first century?

ED—It could be, but there will undoubtedly be variations on its hue.

BM—To what extent are race relations a power struggle?

ED—The relationship between blacks and whites is grounded to some extent in a struggle for power. That prespective helps us understand parts of the dynamic, but certainly not all of it.

BM—I have heard it argued that blacks have a stake in their status as victims. In some perverse way, it gives them an edge in the power game.

ED—I think that is a fanciful view. Victim status sooner or later demoralizes, and I can't see how anyone could recommend demoralization to improve race relations.

BM—I have the impression that the social sciences have not done a very good job of studying racial questions.

ED—I would be inclined to say the social sciences generally have not done a good job of studying anything. We have not really learned much about the social world in recent decades. And I speak as a putative social scientist. At any rate, it is certainly true with respect to racial matters. As the sociologist William Julius Wilson, who just wrote a good book called *The Truly Disadvantaged: The Inner City, the Underclass, and Public Policy*, has said, race means something very different today than it meant 50 or even 20 years ago. We need to plumb its contemporary significance both in broad political, economic, and sociological terms and in terms of everyday relationships among individual human beings. In this light, I find it ironic that some of the most compelling and popular recent fiction on race has not been about the present, but about the past. *The Color Purple* and

Beloved are examples.

BM—Why do you think the social sciences have done such a poor job?

ED—It gets back to what I was saying about not distinguishing carefully between individuals and groups. In our search to generalize we sometimes imply, or allow our readers to infer, that what is true of blacks as a group is true of blacks as individuals. Our studies on race are dominated by national aggregate statistics which compare blacks as a group with whites as a group. But to my knowledge, we have done relatively little of late to examine how individual blacks live their lives in contemporary America. I think we have a pretty good, even though oversimplified, idea of what race meant for people, especially black people, who grew up under desegregation. Talk to any black person of my generation or earlier, and he or she can recall the specific incident which caused the significance of race to be permanently seared into his or her consciousness. But what does race mean for someone growing up today in Fairfax County or Dayton or Houston? And this has policy implications. What appears to be a serious issue from a national perspective may not be a serious issue everywhere, and the solutions that work in, say, Dallas may not work in, say, Detroit. I fear the social sciences have put methodological questions over questions of social substance. Consequently, they are running in ever-narrowing concentric circles. One of my former professors calls this the woodshop syndrome. You go into your woodshop to build a chair, but discover that some of the tools need sharpening, so you start improving the tools, then developing instruments to assess the quality of the tools. By the time all of the materials are ready for use, you have forgotten why you needed them.

BM—A parable for our times and a good note to end on. Would you like to make a final point?

ED—I'll leave you with a question. Is our failure to deal with the problem of race a result of denial or the result of an overt struggle for power? □

An Interview with
GEORGIE ANNE GEYER on

Education
for Global Understanding

GEORGIE ANNE GEYER graduated from Northwestern University and began her career in journalism with the *Chicago Daily News*.
She is now a syndicated columnist on international affairs and a
regular on such television shows as "Washington Week in Review,"
"Meet the Press," and "Firing Line." Ms. Geyer has traveled around
the world numerous times and, in addition to her regular column, has
published several books. There aren't many public figures in
America today who have her grasp of international problems or her
ability to articulate their intricacies.

I was reminded as we talked in her apartment near the Watergate
Hotel in Washington, of a remark I once heard Norman Cousins
make to the effect that the first sign of sanity in these trying times is to
develop a global consciousness. Cousins made his remark in the
context of a conversation we were having about the founders of the
American Republic. I had asked him what he thought their greatest
disappointment would be should they return to our midst today. He
contrasted the universalist intent of the founders with our national
parochialism. The founders, Cousins told me, "saw the United States
as a universal and not merely a national enterprise. For them,

where the human race was going was paramount. They were trying to create a situation in which human beings could fulfill a nobler destiny. We ought never separate ourselves from questions concerning our common human destiny."

I began my interview with Geyer by referring to a column she had recently written on the environment as perhaps our most important foreign policy issue. "We pretend that the old politics is holding," she had written, "although already the need for a new ecological politics is upon us. Non-territorial issues so profound in their import that we can scarcely bear to face them confound even those few thinkers who recognize them. There are virtually no international organizations to deal with these issues, although they are bursting forth everywhere." She cited some examples: The civil war in El Salvador is the world's first overpopulation war; in Haiti, where there is almost no arable land left, we have the world's first total ecological disaster; the West African country of Mauritania may become the first country in modern times to die an ecological death. "In foreign policy terms," she said, "the problem is not only that we are wantonly exhausting the earth, but that we have no international mechanisms or institutions to deal with problems that do not adhere to national borders or governments. Spreading deserts, polluted air, and thinning ozone layers do not offer passports when they cross borders; they are the ghostly wraiths of worlds we begin to know intellectually but still do not see."

I linked her remarks to another of her recent columns, this one on creativity. "The problem you outline," I said, "is surely going to call for creative efforts on a massive scale." "It is," she responded, "and our educational efforts are not adequate to the challenge." I asked her who she would hold up as an exemplary creative thinker. She mentioned the Indonesian diplomat and educator Soejatmoko (he uses only one name). Soejatmoko's argument is that we need international governance rather than international government. "I agree with him," Geyer said, "when he speaks of the need for transnational institutions that can hold governments accountable for their actions to act on global, regional, and humanitarian issues."

Our conversation continued in that vein.

BM—Not many people have seen as much of the world as you have. Do you still travel a lot?

GAG—I want to, but I have been writing a book on Fidel Castro, and that has kept me cooped up this past year. I am dying to get back to traveling.

BM—Where do you want to go next?

GAG—Back to Latin America.

BM—Is that your first love?

GAG—I think it must be. It was where I first went as a young correspondent in 1964, and I keep writing books about it.

BM—What do you think is the reason for your attraction to Latin America?

GAG—It must be the North-South thing, the natural attraction of opposites. But of course, I can't really explain it.

BM—Where after Latin America would you like to go?

GAG—Probably the Soviet Union.

BM—Judging from some of the things you have written, you don't seem to care much for that part of the world.

GAG—I have deep love for Mother Russia, for her history and the churches and the people and the literature. But I certainly don't have any great love for the Soviet bureaucracy. Every morning you have to steel yourself. You get up and tell yourself that you just have to get through the day somehow. But I expect that may have changed. This trip could be quite different.

BM—Glasnost?

GAG—Well, that; but the country in general is becoming much more sophisticated. It used to be just one insult after another. So much so that many times I would just get up and walk away. After all, I am from the south side of Chicago.

BM—Is there any part of the world you haven't covered?

GAG—I've been about everywhere, although some places not as much as I would like. India, for example. But I've been everywhere at least once.

BM—Will you ever tire of traveling?

GAG—I can't imagine it. My happiest moments are when they close the plane doors and I am off again.

BM—What is the secret of writing a good column?

GAG—Keeping close to the beat. I think of the column as a form of reporting. If I get too far away from that, I lose contact and the column becomes abstract. I never go back to a country, even a country that I know very well, like Egypt, expecting to find what I found before. It's always different. And the legwork has be done all over again—gathering the facts, reading history, doing the interviews.

That never stops, nor should it. There is always something new. I only make mistakes when I forget that.

BM—Do you still think of yourself as a foreign correspondent?

GAG—A syndicated columnist on international affairs might be more accurate. Or perhaps a foreign correspondent who writes opinion.

BM—Let's talk about journalism's role in our society for a while. You have written that journalists have become "the arbiters of truth" in our society. Some think they have become something like Plato's philosopher-kings who advise and even control the powerful and tell us which way the world is tilting.

GAG—That might be a hard case to make. It would certainly come as a surprise to many journalists. Journalism is basically a craft. We don't even have the credentials to be a profession. But we are a craft that has become a tremendous power. And this has happened within the span of my own career. When I started out in journalism with the *Chicago Daily News* in 1959, I was the first college-educated reporter on the paper. I was also the first woman. The others were all white males who had come from the street. They were excellent reporters and wonderful people. But they didn't take themselves too seriously, certainly not as philosopher-kings. Today, many young reporters go into journalism with the idea of changing the world, and often with the intention of becoming celebrities. This worries me very much.

BM—Why?

GAG—Because I have the impression no one is thinking much about this tremendous power journalists have acquired. Many of them would deny it altogether. There is a tendency to wear the responsibility very lightly. Consequently, there is a lot of irresponsible reporting. I noticed that just recently in the coverage of the Persian Gulf. I wrote a column about how skewed the first reports of events there were. They said a ship had hit a mine, we had lost, it was all over. Well, you can't cover as many wars and revolutions as I have and say it is all over in one day. This is very superficial and puts negative attitudes up front. So journalists don't tend to be very intellectual. But I did write that they have become the arbiters of truth because a funny thing has happened in our society. Lots of original thinking is going on, many creative things are being done, but the public only becomes aware of them when they have passed through the conduit of the media.

Journalism has become a kind of filter through which all opinions must pass to gain a public hearing. That may be good. Or it may be bad. But we ought to think it through. Most journalists absolutely refuse to think about the social consequences of their work. That comes up from time to time in our professional meetings. I remember someone once suggested that we ought to have a consequences editor on our papers. It was intended as a joke, but I am inclined to take that idea seriously.

BM—Still, many of the best practitioners of the craft are very thoughtful.

GAG—A minority only.

BM—Are journalism schools improving the situation?

GAG—Not as far as I can see. In the journalism schools, it's all nuts and bolts. But we don't need any more surveys of how many words should go into a headline. I saw a report recently that said most journalism professors were never practicing journalists. We are a craft, and yet people teaching it haven't practiced the craft. That's scary because I have seen time and time again how other countries manipulate us through our press, countries like Iran and Nicaragua who do not wish us well. They know how to time stories. They know when to hold press conferences. They are adept at controlling news releases. And most of them know us very well. They have studied here and have observed us more closely than we have observed them or even have observed ourselves. They play to our media rhythms which are the pulse beat of our whole society. I don't think anyone has done a study of how newscasts, or even newsbreaks, shape Americans' character and outlooks.

BM—What do you recommend?

GAG—I don't understand why journalists haven't taken Marshall McLuhan's ideas about communication more seriously. I think I would start by assigning some of his writings.

BM—Chesterton once said that journalism was the most democratic of all the professions because it was direct communication between the intellectuals and the public.

GAG—A nice thought. But we don't seem to have an intellectual class of that nature. A book published recently complains about that, claiming that there are no writers or thinkers who address a general and educated audience, people like Mary McCarthy, Dwight Macdonald and Edmund Wilson of an earlier generation. If you have any thoughts on that question, let me know because it is a question that concerns me very much. Someday I would like to put some things together.

BM—At least your own columns do great credit to the craft. Someone has said your columns are to the print media what the "MacNeil/Lehrer News Hour" is to the electronic media.

GAG—That's too kind.

BM—Let's come now to your area of expertise. Latin America always seems so puzzling to Americans, a mystery wrapped in an enigma, as Winston Churchill might have said. Why do we have so much difficulty understanding Latin America?

GAG—It's our education basically. We've heard criticisms of our educational system in general but it is particularly woeful with respect to international understanding. If I were a student today, I would rise up in protest against the kind of education that is being offered.

BM—Say a little more about that.

GAG—If I were a student today, I would say, "Don't do this to me. Don't turn me out as a mediocre, uncreative, uninformed person. You haven't made me understand the world because you have taken the easy way out. You've given me what I said I wanted, but it wasn't really what I wanted."

BM—Do you speak much to students?

GAG—Yes, a fair amount. I am respectful of them, but I am also very tough with them.

BM—What kinds of questions do they ask you?

GAG—Most often, they ask me what they should be preparing for. They ask, "What is society looking for? What should we be?" I tell them that is the wrong question. I tell them to be what they want to be, to follow their love. Another question I get frequently, and it is a revealing one, is, "Ms. Geyer, how do you control your interviews?" The question of control is very important to young people today.

BM—How do you answer that?

GAG—I tell them the answer is very simple: I have to know more than the person I am interviewing. If I don't, I can be used and victimized. Students always give me a funny look when I tell them that. But they think about it a while and agree that it makes sense. That seems to me an effective way of making the point that knowledge is important, and that is what education is all about.

BM—You had a good line in one of your columns to the effect that life should be a dedication rather than a pastime. That is a good message for students to hear. Too many of them seem to think life is a game on Wall Street or something like that.

GAG—Thank you.

BM—Was your own education adequate preparation for your career?

GAG—What I had was very good, but I didn't have enough of it. Public schools weren't very good in Chicago, but I was so hungry for education that I really threw myself into it. And I loved Northwestern.

BM—What did you study there?

GAG—My best courses were in history, politics and government, literature, and, of course, journalism. If I had to do it all over again, I would, in addition to those subjects, take courses in philosophy, science, anthropology, sociology, and languages. I didn't have any of those in college.

BM—How were your journalism courses?

GAG—Of the nuts and bolts variety. And I regret that. In fact, I regretted it then. Those things you can learn very easily on the job.

BM—Ted Fiske, who is the education editor of The New York Times, said he never took a course in journalism and wouldn't recommend anyone else do it either.

GAG—I can see his point.

BM—What should students study to understand Latin America?

GAG—First of all, history.

BM—The history of the whole continent, each and every country?

GAG—Absolutely. Cultural history. Political history. Economic history. And comparative history of the Spanish and Portuguese. Next in importance are languages.

BM—Could you tell us in 25 words or less what is going on in Latin America? Is any progress being made there?

GAG—Definitely. There is tremendous progress and tremendous change. But if you don't have a historical perspective, you can't know that. From week to week, or even from year to year, it looks the same.

BM—To some, it looks the same from century to century.

GAG—But it doesn't. Not even from decade to decade. One change that is clear is the evolution from feudalism to democractic, or at least representative, forms of government.

BM—What countries are in the vanguard in that respect?

GAG—Mexico is the oldest. Mexico took a giant step toward representative government early in the century. Costa Rica and

Venezuela did it a long time ago. El Salvador and Nicaragua are at a critical point right now. The countries that had the most rigid Spanish and aristocractic structures are having the most trouble. Colombia and Peru would be examples.

BM—What is the most economically advanced Latin American country?

GAG—Again, Mexico. At least until recently, but I think they will pull out of their present difficulties. And, again, Costa Rica and Venezuela, which have always been among the most democratic of Latin American countries. Ironically, Honduras is in pretty good economic shape, partly because it had no large land tracts and everyone was poor. So everyone could rise together. They are a nice people and a democractic people. Guatemala, on the other hand, has had a strong aristocratic tradition, and that is very hard to break down.

BM—Are you implying that democracy is the inevitable wave of the future in Latin America?

GAG—The political history of Latin America is cyclical. It alternates between representative government and military takeovers. But to the trained eye, there are perceptible gains in the cycles. Now and again, a military regime disappears from the cycle as it did in Peru in 1968. So in that time frame, I see a progressive curve. There are casualties, of course, and some people lose, but in the aggregate people are better educated and economically better off. Part of the explanation is that people want more. That is part of the problem as well because as the progressive curve goes up, violence sometimes escalates. So there is a kind of formula according to which the higher the expectations, the more intense the violence. That is the tragedy of the recent history of El Salvador. At one point, El Salvador was doing so well that it was called the Taiwan of Latin America.

BM—What happened?

GAG—Several things converged more or less at the same time. Massive overpopulation has always been a problem in that country. Then there was the soccer war in 1968. Then several hundred thousand Salvadorans were thrown back from Honduras and settled around the big cities, where they soon became dispirited, perfect fodder for guerrilla warfare. Finally, the political system collapsed. When Duarte and the Christian Democrats came to power in 1972, there was a moment of hope, and it could have been the occasion of momentous change. But the old rightist military faction counter-reacted, and that is when everything became poisonous. It will take years for that country to come back.

BM—To the untutored eye, it all looks a mess. It is good to know that you discern a line of progress and hope in all the turmoil.

GAG—I really do.

BM—Still, it remains true that democracy does not come easily to Latin Ameria.

GAG—No. It doesn't. But it is coming. Look at Mother Spain. That is also a great hope.

BM—Do Latin Americans still look to Spain as a mother?

GAG—The point I was making is that they have such similar structures that if Spain can democratize, then so can Latin America.

BM—But at the price of revolution?

GAG—It may well be a very high price. It already is in some countries.

BM—So revolution is inevitable?

GAG—It certainly seems to be.

BM—Is it worth it?

GAG—It doesn't really matter if it is inevitable. If the old Right won't relase some power, there will be revolution. Of course, another thing is that there isn't much old Right anymore. What we have to worry about now is the new Left. I hated Somoza, and then I discovered I didn't like the Sandinistas either. And then I was unhappy with myself for not liking the Sandinistas. So I thought about it and told myself, "No, you don't have to be unhappy with yourself. Just because you didn't like the old dictators of the Right, doesn't mean you have to like the new dictators of the Left." Many people can't make that intellectual jump. They think that if they didn't like the old, they are under some moral obligation to like the new regime, even though it might be every bit as bad as the old.

BM—There doesn't seem to be any middle way in Latin America, and the middle way is the way of democracy. Doesn't the absence of mediating institutions make the cause of democracy much more difficult?

GAG—They are building up. And that is a source of hope. Interestingly enough, the inspiration for democratic reform comes from the United States, and the economic aid comes from us, but the political help and training comes from the Europeans, from the Christian Democrats and Social Democrats in France and Spain and especially in Germany. They give enormous amounts of money and training to their counterparts in Latin America. That is what is really building democracy there. Under the European influence, they are doing a really remarkable job of building up the center Left. Every Christian Democrat in Latin America, and that is the party of change, has been trained by the European influence.

BM—Is this a missionary effort on the part of European countries?

GAG—No, it is strictly through the parties. They have extensive contacts back and forth. The Socialist International, which is a wing of the Socialist Democractic Party, has great influence.

BM—Is there a fairly strong Marxist component in the European influence?

GAG—No, not from Europe. Strange as it may seem, it is those who are most rooted in the old Hispanic, authoritarian mind-set who make the transition to Marxism most easily.

BM—Maybe not so strange when you consider they are going from one form of feudalism to another. Many think Marxism is an updated form of feudalism.

GAG—Exactly. A kind of international feudalism.

BM—One would think they would look more to America than Europe for help in putting in place democratic institutions.

GAG—They do. Inside. Their anger and rage at us can be explained psychologically by the fact that they expect so much from us and we let them down so often. We so often and so stupidly move to frustrate in them precisely what we have inspired.

BM—A telling point. Does liberation theology have an influence on the democratic movement in Latin America?

GAG—That is very complicated. What decent person does not want to see the lot of the poor improved? Who is not for liberation? But what does all that mean in practice? I was the first American to write about liberation theology back in 1965 and 1966. There are certainly some good ideas in the movement. The idea of base Christian communities is a fine one. But in truth, I don't see liberation theology having the answer because there is nothing in it about the creation of wealth.

BM—That is what the theologian Michael Novak has been saying.

GAG—I agree with him on that. Novak hits the praxis question very hard. When people ask me, "Will liberation theology work?" I answer that what works is individual initiative. And there is plenty of individual initiative in Latin America. The poor are no longer passive observers of their state. I don't think liberation theology helps them become creatively engaged with improving their lot. It can make them very dissatisfied with their lot, but doing something about it is another matter. People say, "Well, creating wealth is all very Protestant and Northern and capitalistic." And it is. But it is the best solution to poverty we know.

BM—How would you grade the efforts of the American government in Latin America?

GAG—Most American diplomats I have known there have been sympathetic to democratic reforms. It is only the people in the top echelons who have supported the Somozas and the Batistas.

BM—But isn't that where the real power is? Isn't it decisions at the top that count in the end?

GAG—I am not so sure. Our embassies have given a lot of help to the democractic reformers. In all fairness to President Reagan, he is supporting the democrats in Central America even though many of his people would love to have the hard Right back. But it isn't coming back. That is how history changes things. The Somozas were spawned by conditions of a certain time and place which have now passed by. By the same logic the Soviet Union could never go back to Stalin. It is a different country now. There is more education and more freedom.

BM—So you support Reagan's stand on the contras?

GAG—I have hesitantly and without enthusiasm supported it. In the beginning, I supported the Sandinistas. They were a great movement, and they overthrew Somoza. But I don't think you can call them Sandinistas anymore. Their top leadership is hard-line authoritarian; they want total power, and they love their position on the world stage. The more they are attacked in this country, the more they feel they have come into their manhood. I don't think they are good for Nicaragua, I don't think the Soviet and Cuban influence is good, and I don't think they are good for their neighbors. I was begging to get Somoza out in time. You might say I was prematurely anti-Somoza. My record is very clean on that, and my liberal credentials are in good order, so I can in good conscience speak favorably of the contras. They have protected the other democracies in Central America, and they have turned the Sandinistas' impulses to expansion inward. At a terrible cost. It breaks my heart. But as a result of the contra opposition, the Sandinistas may have to liberalize somewhat because they have failed so terribly.

BM—Have you interviewed Ortega?

GAG—Yes.

BM—What were your impressions?

GAG—I interviewed him the week after he came into power. As with all revolutions, the immediate aftermath was ecstatic. I spent three hours with him one afternoon, and I found him to be a very intelligent person. I quoted what he said to me widely. He told me the situation in Nicaragua would not be like the Cuban revolution, that his party had a *compromiso*, a kind of compact with or promise to the people. There were, he pointed out, many groups represented in the revolution besides the Sandinistas. There were Catholics, Marxists, opposition figures, Christian Democrats, and Protestants. "This will be a truly democratic regime that reflects the interests of all the people," Ortega told me that afternoon.

BM—Did you believe him?

GAG—I wanted to believe him. But things didn't turn out as Ortega said they would. And it can't be argued that the United States drove Ortega into his extreme position. The analogy with Cuba doesn't hold. After all, he had 18 months of Jimmy Carter, who practically wanted to give him the East Wing of the White House. In the beginning, we were all very sympathetic and hopeful. Ortega could have retained power and at the same time had a reasonably democratic state. That was a clear option. The stupidity of it all is that he went so far to the Left.

BM—Why do you think he did?

GAG—I attribute it to the desire for glory.

BM—A good old-fashioned aristocratic virtue.

GAG—Indeed.

BM—Do you think the contras have much of a chance?

GAG—I just don't know. I've tried to think that through, and it is very murky. I am amazed that they have anyone fighting with them at all. After all, Ortega is not a hated dictator. You don't have the kind of corruption you had with Somoza. What you have is a stupid collectivist regime that can't do anything efficiently and antagonizes everyone. The Nicaraguan people really want a democratic government. That is more and more true all over Latin America today. And I suppose that is why people are still fighting with the contras.

BM—The fact that there isn't much grass-roots support for them in this country is probably an instance of what you said earlier about letting them down.

GAG—Unfortunately, I think that is the case.

BM—Would you say Ortega is the most extreme leader in Latin America now?

GAG—No. Ortega is really quite a weak leader. He is far from a charismatic leader, and that is one reason why his government is falling apart. When he speaks, for example, he mimics Castro all the time. And God knows I know Castro's every gesture. Castro is definitely the most charismatic leader in Latin America. They say Alan Garcia in Peru is now, but I haven't been down there since he came to power. Most Latin American leaders are calm, rational, and smart. That is another sign of hope. As I often say jokingly, I don't need my sex objects waving to a crowd from a balcony.

BM—You said at the beginning of the interview that you were writing a book on Castro. How's it going?

GAG—Painfully.

BM—Is Castro cooperating with you?

GAG—No. Not at all. The last time I was in Cuba we had a big argument. Now he won't let me into the country.

BM—Why do you think another book on Castro is needed now?

GAG—Well it may not be needed, but I am writing it because, for one thing, I know a lot about him; but, more deeply, Castro launched a unique political experiment in Latin America.

BM—Has it been successful?

GAG—Cuba changed after 1959. No doubt about that. But in many ways, they changed backwards. For example, they are impoverished compared to where they were in the 1950s. Economically, Cuba is an absolutely dependent state.

BM—What do you think will happen in Cuba? Will Castro hang on indefinitely?

GAG—There is no serious internal opposition to him, although there have been several very high-level defections recently. But what is significant, and what really frightens Castro, is that he is losing his hold on the people. In fact, he may already have lost it. I have a chapter in my book called "The Spell," which refers to the ability he had to hold audiences entranced for hours. I've even talked to psychiatrists about this trait. But everything indicates that Castro is losing it, and that he knows he is losing it. The young are bored with him. They have a word to describe him which means "Old grandma." Cuban youth want the good things of the world just like the young Soviets do. They want jobs, they want to travel, they want normal comforts. But to answer your question, yes, I suppose Castro will hang on. He is such a tactical genius that he has everything sewed up. The controls are so tight. That is why he has never been assassinated. He has such an incredible control group around him. But he's losing touch. I've also noticed that he has aged markedly in recent months.

BM—How do the psychiatrists assess Castro's personality?

GAG—He is very much like his father, whom he hated. His father was a very uncultured man, as Fidel is. He is educated but not cultured. He hates anything to do with culture, just as Hitler did. His father came from Spain and went to a remote area of Cuba where he became very wealthy and took over large tracts of land by moving the fences at night. Fidel has done something similar. He has moved Cuba's fences all over the world. He is the leader of a small country that has no economic base, and yet he is a world power. The man has got to be a genius.

BM—How would you compare the democratic prospects in Latin America to other Third World countries?

GAG—Back in the sixties, when I first went there, we used to say that of all the underdeveloped countries in the world, Latin America had the best chance if making it because it was Christian and it was Western. Now that judgment is challenged by many because the areas that are making it seem to be in the Pacific rim, which is neither Christian nor Western.

BM—Pacific countries have made it economically, but they don't seem to have made great democratic strides.

GAG—That is still my opinion, too. So I stick by my earlier judgment that Latin America has the best chance.

BM—Do you think the American press is doing a good job of getting the story on Latin America out?

GAG—Within strict limits. The reporting has become much more accurate. But as I travel around the country, I don't see much of it. TV is quick to report the more dramatic, bang-bang type events, but when the wars die down, the media lose interest. Reporters find that their stories don't get printed when there is no battle coverage. This means that the political story isn't getting told. This limited kind of coverage gives the American people the impression that there is war all of the time in Central America when, as a matter of fact, there is no fighting about 90 percent of the time.

BM—Would the American people become more enlightened about Latin American affairs if there were better media coverage?

GAG—Better media coverage couldn't hurt. But one thing that troubles me about so many Americans is their romantic infatuation with places like Nicaragua because of its "revolution." Most Americans haven't got the foggiest notion of what a revolution is like. It certainly isn't a very pleasant thing. But Americans like the romance of revolution, and I frankly think a lot of them like it because it is against the United States. It really troubles me that so many otherwise liberal-minded Americans fawn all over the Sandinistas while they won't give the Democrats the time of day or appreciate the fact that they are doing the hard nitty-gritty work that is necessary to build a democratic society. Last year, when I was in El Salvador, I visited one of the Catholic bishops. He told me they had just received their first official visit from the American Catholic hierarchy. But they have been to Nicaragua. Nicaragua is filled with Catholics and Protestants supporting the Sandinistas. Something is very odd here. I think they really ought to think about what they are supporting.

BM—We'll end on that note. Thank you very much for a generous interview. □

An Interview with
HENRY GIROUX on

The Dream of
Radical Education

THE School of Education at Miami University in Oxford, Ohio, is
housed in McGuffey Hall, named after the author of the famous
nineteenth-century readers and a long-time professor at Miami University. As one approaches the building from the west, a large statue
of McGuffey rears from the shrubbery. The inscription reads:

Wm. Holmes McGuffey
1800-1878
Who while professor in Miami University
compiled the famous McGuffey readers
Which established the social standards
of the great Middle West of the United States.
Eminent Divine and Philosopher
Peer of College Teachers
Inspirer of young men

On another panel are chiseled the first words from the first lesson
of the first McGuffey reader:

Here is John
And there are Ann and John.
Ann has got a new book.

Ann must keep it nice and clean.
John must not tear the book.
But he may see how fast he can learn.

It was both appropriate and ironic that Henry Giroux, a leading spokesperson for radical education in America today, should have his offices in a building named after McGuffey—appropriate because both attained a measure of recognition in the educational world and ironic because one could scarely imagine two more dissimilar philosophies. When we met Giroux in his third floor offices, he commented on the irony. "McGuffey was pretty conservative in his thinking, but he was a committed educator. We share that in common. Let me point out another irony," Giroux said, "When I was at Boston University, President John Silber and I shared an interest in and appreciation of McGuffey. Silber really liked him. But that didn't count for much when I got fired." He chuckled, as though, in retrospect, he relished the experience. "I have lots of critics," he went on and showed me an article from the *National Review* he had pinned to his bulletin board in which his book *Education Under Siege* was roundly denounced. I told him that it was probably good for his career that he had critics in such high places.

But I had not come to talk about critics or about McGuffey. I wanted to get some perspective on a movement in education that is gaining considerable prominence in our national debate, so I began with a question to that point.

BM—What is radical education?

HG—Radical education doesn't refer to a discipline or a body of knowledge. It suggests a particular kind of practice and a particular posture of questioning received institutions and received assumptions. I would say in a general way that the basic premises of radical education grew out of the crisis in social theory. More specifically, we can distinguish three traits: Radical education is interdisciplinary in nature, it questions the fundamental categories of all disciplines, and it has a public mission of making society more democratic. This last point is perhaps the principal reason why radical education as a field is so exciting. We can take ideas and apply them.

BM—Almost like having your own laboratory?

HG—Something like that. I prefer to think of it as a public sphere. Most disciplines don't have that. As a result, their attempts to construct a public discourse become terribly academized and limited.

That is why I find radical education so exciting both theoretically and politically.

BM—How close is the tie between the two?

HG—Very close. We can add that as another distinguishing trait. Radical education joins theory and praxis.

BM—Is radical synonymous with critical?

HG—Yes, I think they have to be. I can't conceive of a radical position that is not at the same time, and even in the first instance, critical both in historical terms about the ways schools have evolved in this country and ideologically in terms of the particular kinds of values that operate in our schools and in our practices of education. Critical education operates on two basic assumptions. One, there is a need for a language of critique, a questioning of presuppositions. Radical educators, for example, criticize and, indeed, reject the notion that the primary purpose of public education is economic efficiency. Schools are more than company stores. They have the much more radical purpose of educating citizens, which is why the second basic assumption of radical education is a language of possibility. It goes beyond critique to elaborate a positive language of human empowerment.

BM—We hear a lot about empowerment these days. How do you understand that term?

HG—It is the ability to think and act critically. This notion has a double reference: to the individual and to society. The freedom and human capacities of individuals must be developed to their maximum, but individual powers must be linked to democracy in the sense that social betterment must be the necessary consequence of individual flourishing. Radical educators look upon schools as social forms. Those forms should educate the capacities people have to think, to act, to be subjects, and to be able to understand the limits of their ideological commitments. That's a radical paradigm. Radical educators believe that the relationship between social forms and social capacities is such that human capacities get educated to the point of calling into question the forms themselves. What the dominant educational philosophies want is to educate people to adapt to those social forms rather than critically interrogate them. Democracy is a celebration of difference, the politics of difference, I call it, and the dominant philosophies fear this.

BM—Is your position that our assumptions were at one time sound and became outmoded, or were they faulty to begin with?

HG—If we are talking about traditional perspectives, I think the traditionalists have always been wrong about the nature of education.

BM—How can you say such a thing?

HG—Let me put it differently and say that within the field of education the languages that have dominated have generally been languages that have highly instrumentalized the purposes of schooling by either privileging certain groups of elites who become the managers of society or narrowing the scope of education so severely that schools become mere factories to train the work force. The traditionalists lack a language of possibiliity about how schools can play a major role in shaping public life.

BM—But surely the liberal arts tradition has not been instrumentalist in that way?

HG—I say that liberal education in any ideal sense of that term has always occupied a subordinate position vis-à-vis the dominant languages. And that is unquestionably true in this country since the 1950s. If we are talking about the public schools, then the instrumentalist argument is very, very powerful. And this has been true from the beginning. If we are talking about higher education, then it depends on what kinds of schools we have in mind. We all know our educational system is tiered. Some institutions are vocational. Others are places of real learning, although primarily for the elite. Harvard will never define itself as an institution whose primary mission is the promotion of industrial growth! It appeals to the life of the mind, the good life, and so forth. The higher rhetoric! We can distinguish different missions. But if we look at higher education in general, I argue that the instrumentalist ideology prevails.

BM—Hasn't the wave of reforms we have had lessened the dominance of that ideology?

HG—I don't think so. Most of them have to my way of thinking been misguided. What has been the thrust of these reforms? Back to basics, merit pay, a standardized curriculum, raising test scores, evaluation criteria, and the like. This is just another version of the technological fix that ignores the philosophical questions. It is quantifying the educational process in a belief that the outcome will be some kind of excellence or economic competence. All of this suggests to me that those who are pushing these reforms have no educational philosophy at all. We have to ask what the purposes of education are, what kind of citizens we hope to produce. To say that test scores are the answer is to beg the question of "What do test scores measure anyway?"

Here is a story that perfectly illustrates the point. Joe Clark, a school principal in Newark, has been touted by many reformers as the paragon of what an inner-school educator should be. How does Clark operate? He marches through the halls of his school with a bullhorn and a baseball bat, publicly berating anybody who flouts his authority. When student misbehave they must learn the school anthem and sing it over the P.A. system. Clark is given credit for restoring authority to the school and for raising the test scores of his students. What that report omits is that some 900 students, most of them minorities, have been expelled to roam the streets with bleak prospects. One has to ask, What educational philosophy motivates this kind of action? What sense of learning do students get? How do teachers teach in such a context?

BM—Has there ever been a time when schools met your criteria?

HG—No, although there is a discernible tradition of dissent and vision that argues for a connection with the imperatives of a critical democracy. It is an important and powerful tradition, particularly during the 1920s and 1930s in this country. But we are not talking about much history here. Prior to the twentieth century there wasn't much education of the sort we think appropriate for a democracy for the simple reason there wasn't much democracy.

BM—Does democracy have to be critical democracy to be genuine?

HG—That's what I mean. Dewey talked about democracy as a way of life that has to be made and remade by each generation.

BM—The existentialists use the word appropriation to cover all questions of making our ideals meaningful in a lived context.

HG—I like that word. It brings to the fore for me the crucial role of pedagogy and the question of how we learn to become subjects who engage not only our own self-formation but the possibilities for society at any given time. How does one come to self-understanding? How does one situate oneself in history? How do we relate questions of knowledge to power? How do we understand the limitations of our institutions, or even of our age? Those are pedagogical questions. Radical educators understand them to be political questions as well. But let's face it, this is a lost discourse. None of the many recent reports about educational reform even scratches the surface of this problem.

BM—What problem is that again?
HG—The relationship betwen pedagogy and power.
BM—How do you assess Bennett's tenure as secretary of education?
HG—I give Bennett credit for putting education front and center on the national agenda. Education has become one of our most exciting debates. Bennett has both politicized and polarized that debate. It should have been politicized but not polarized. Still, as a result, many have had to come to critical grips with their common-sense assumptions about what schooling is. For that I applaud Bennett. He has initiated a terrific dialogue. But having said that, I want to make it clear that I have no respect for his opinions.
BM—None of them?
HG—None at all. There is nothing that he has said that suggests he has anything positive to offer for a theory of education. He follows a policy that resembles our immigration policies in the 1920s and 1930s, a policy that doesn't rest upon a serious theory of public life and denies the politics of difference. The values Bennett espouses are authority, elitism, and cultural uninformity.
BM—But Bennett has fought hard against anti-intellectualism.
HG—It is a fact that anti-intellectualism in American education is rampant, influencing even those whose intentions are actually opposed to the closing of the doors to genuine learning. We know that the environment in most universities is inimical to broadly based, philosophically informed scholarship and dialogue concerning burning questions of politics and culture. In a few places, liberal and radical intellectuals are building micro-institutions (centers, institutes, programs) within the universities as outposts that attempt to resist the larger trends toward instrumentalized curricula. These programs wisely accept that they are engaged in an intellectual as well as political project, but, for the most part, their influence is confined to the already initiated. I don't think Bennett has the cure for anti-intellectualism.
BM—Are radical educators a heard voice in the land?
HG—They are an argument on the block, especially since 1976 when Samuel Bowles and Herbert Gintis published their path-breaking *Schooling in Capitalist Society.* I would argue that that book, along with some seminal works in the sociology of education, provided the foundation for a new language that went beyond the earlier critical tradition of Dewey and his colleagues. In the last 10

years, this influence has become quite evident in what is published, what is taught, and what is talked about at professional meetings.

BM—Does radical education draw its inspiration primarily from Marxism?

HG—It did. Bowles and Gintis did. But as I look at the work of radical educators today, I would find it difficult to say that Marxism is the primary influence on it. And where the Marxist influence exists, it is pretty crude stuff.

BM—You mean not good Marxism?

HG—It is more a question of how good Marxism is to begin with. We can appropriate a number of good things from Marxism, but do we want to appropriate the paradigm itself?

BM—It seems the radical educator has to do just that in some sense because Marxism has supplied the principal language of critique in the twentieth century. Where else would you look?

HG—I would say that to be a radical educator today you have to engage the Marxist tradition. And there is no question that Marxist discourse dominated in the beginning because in the beginning most work in radical education was about reproduction theory.

BM—What is that?

HG—It is a Marxist category which says that the basic functions of the schools is to reproduce the dictates of the state in the economic order. It was a rather simple and mechanistic view, but not entirely false, and it had important consequences for politicizing the debate about the purpose of schools, which is something that the paradigm itself completely ignored.

BM—But are there other traditions?

HG—I myself draw from a number of positions. There are critical traditions in feminist literature, in literary theory, and in liberation theology that I find useful. But it is hard to put a label on all of this. I would like to call myself a good working-class, radical American.

BM—As in populist?

HG—Sure. A critical populist who includes some elements of the IWW, Bill Haywood, C. Wright Mills, Martin Luther King, and Michael Harrington. In other words, people who speak to people in a language that dignifies their history and their experience. I don't understand how you can speak to people if you don't celebrate their voices.

BM—How did you become interested in this field?

HG—I went to college on a basketball scholarship. I started off in the sciences, but then the Vietnam War came along and all of a sudden social theory become very important. The more I read the more I became interested in teaching. Not only did I see that as a way to make an impact, but I saw teaching as a wonderfully noble profession. And I still feel that way. One of the things I try to impress upon my students is how important this field is.

BM—What did you do your Ph.D. dissertation on?

HG—It was a study of curriculum. I was interested in the different ways kids learn in schools and the ways in which subject matters get selected for the curriculum. Where I grew up, learning was a collective activity. But when I got to school and tried to share learning with other students, that was called cheating. The curriculum sent the clear message to me that learning was a highly individualistic, almost secretive, endeavor. My working-class experience didn't count. Not only did it not count, it was disparaged. I was being reproduced according to a different logic. I think schools should be about ways of life. They are not simply instruction sites. They are cultures which legitimize certain forms of knowledge and disclaim others. The language for understanding this phenomenon in some pretty sophisticated ways is now starting to emerge.

BM—For example?

HG—Take the work being done on ideology and language in schools. It's very rich. If you believe that language actively constructs as well as reflects social reality, that language always develops out of a sense of difference—if something is this, it is not that—and that language always embodies particular kinds of values, then you can raise questions. You can ask, What is the relationship between what is learned and the pedagogies in place? Where does the language they use come from? Whose interests does it promote? What are its value assumptions? And the like.

BM—One thinks of inner-city schools. It seems to be the case there that the kind of education offered mismatches the experience of those to whom it is offered.

HG—In my mind, we have instrumentalized the process of education so much that we have forgotten that the referent out of which we operate is a white, upper-middle-class logic that not only modulizes but actually silences subordinate voices. If you believe that schooling is about somebody's story, somebody's history, somebody's set of memories, a particular set of experiences, then it is clear that just one logic will not suffice.

BM—*Not many people believe that.*

HG—Well, I'm surprised how many do. Even people of a very conservative cast are much more open to the kind of argument I am making. They, too, see schools as cultural institutions, as cultural frontiers, if you will, and not merely boot camps for the economy. They see the value dimension. Unfortunately, their understanding is not very democratic. I used Bennett as an example a moment ago. My point is that learning has to be meaningful to students before it can become critical. Our problem is that we have a theory of knowledge but no theory of pedagogy.

BM—*Isn't this all pretty abstract? After all, schools are run bureaucratically on the principles of delegated responsibility and dictated policies. And that seems clearly what the majority of Americans want.*

HG—But that's another question altogether, although related to the first question. The first question is, Can learning take place if it in fact silences the voices of the people it is supposed to teach? And the answer is yes. People learn that they don't count. The second question is, What are the necessary conditions to educate teachers to be intellectuals so they can engage critically the relationship between culture and learning and change the conditions under which they work? As I put it in some of my writings, we need to redefine the role of teachers as transformative intellectuals.

BM—*Would you elaborate on that intriguing idea?*

HG—Michael Waltzer speaks of intellectuals as engaged citizens. They do not operate from an aloof perspective that legitmizes the separation of facts from values. They understand the nature of their own self-formation, have some vision of the future, see the importance of education as a public discourse, and have a sense of mission in providing students what they need to become critical citizens. So to give you a somewhat schematic sense of what I mean by teachers as transformative intellectuals, I would say, first, that teachers are engaged. They are partisans, not doctrinaire. They believe something, say what they believe, and offer their belief to others in a framework that always makes it debatable and open to critical inquiry. Second, to talk about teachers as intellectuals is to say they should have an active role in shaping the curriculum. Think of intelligence as a form of currency that enables teachers to have a role in shaping school policy, defining educational philosophies, and working with their communities in a variety of capacities. Transformative intellectuals are aware of their own theoretical convictions and are skilled in strategies for translating them into practice. Above all, finally, it means being able to exercise power. Pedagogy is always related to power. In fact, educational theories, like any philosophy, are ideologies that have an intimate relation to questions of power. So learning must be linked not just to learning in the schools but extended to shaping public life and social relationships. The proletarianization of the teaching profession has made educators too dependent and powerless. Does that give you some idea?

BM—That's fine. Wouldn't you want, for much the same reasons, all professionals to be transformative intellectuals?

HG—To be sure. But bear in mind that the teaching profession alone has the primary responsibility to educate critical citizens, whereas we might argue that the first responsibility of, say, the medical profession, is healing. Educators have a public responsibility that by its very nature involves them in the struggle for democracy. This makes the teaching profession a unique and powerful public resource.

BM—Are schools of education moving toward this thinking?

HG—The short answer is that they are starting to move, but very slowly. And I have to say, without naming names, that some of our most progressive schools of education have become disappointingly reactionary. They tend more and more to hire people in the business manager mode, and there are few, very few, critical voices to be heard.

BM—Talk a little about your teaching experience.

HG—It's both very gratifying and very challenging.

BM—Tell us about the challenging part.

HG—Most of our students are very comfortable with defining themselves as technicians and clerks. For them to be all of a sudden exposed to a line of critical thinking that both calls their own experience into question and at the same time raises fundamental questions about what teaching should be and what social purposes it might serve is very hard for them. They don't have a frame of reference or a vocabulary with which to articulate the centrality of what they do. They are caught up in market logic and bureaucratic jargon. We can't defend what we do that way. We can't make our best case. We always wind up on the defensive and appear to others as second rate and marginal. If, on the other hand, we make the case for critical democracy, we can at the same time make the case for the centrality of the teaching profession. Of one thing I am sure—the older paradigm is dying not only in terms of its effectiveness, but in terms of its legitimacy as well.

BM—That's usually referred to as positivism, and it has been stated more than once that positivism is dead. Yet it seems to be a very lively corpse.

HG—Oh, it's not dead. I am not saying that at all. What you call positivism I would want to call technocratic rationality or scientism, which identifies the idea of progress with an idea of efficiency, which in turn defines itself by abstracting from questions of power and politics and values. What I am saying is that paradigm is breaking down, not dead. Look at the urban school systems. They are falling apart all over the country.

BM—Do you find some teaching techniques more effective than others?

HG—My courses are all seminars. I prescribe the materials I think are important, but the students have to write papers and defend their positions. This is the basis of a 15-week working-through process. I don't care what positions the students take. I want them to be able to justify whatever position they do take so they come out with a clearer sense of what they believe in and what effects that might have. I think what I really do is politicize the process of education in the minds of the students. As soon as you say people can be agents in the act of learning, you politicize the issue of schooling. It becomes political in the best sense of the word, which is to say that students have to become self-conscious about the kinds of social relationships that undergird the learning process. That's a political issue. Another thing I take very seriously in my teaching is illustrating principles with a sense of voice, with somebody's story. There are experiences out there that illuminate larger questions of educational philosophy. We can, for example, talk about the hidden curriculum of racism, about what black kids have to give up to become academically successful, and we can do this through their own voices. Or we can talk about people who have no community of memories. We can talk about people who are defined by such a nonbelief in the common good that they can't even imagine an alternative vision according to anything other than highly individualistic and egotistical norms. Those stories are important. That is one of the reasons I have a lot of trouble with liberal and procedural morality. It eliminates the stories in favor of abstract rules. Of course, we need to understand that these stories by themselves do not always speak for themselves. But they can become the basis for analyzing a whole range of considerations that are often hidden in the stories. Experience never simply speaks for itself. The language that we bring to it determines its meaning.

BM—Speak further to the point about student voices. How do you deal with the objection that students are virtual tabulae rasae *who don't have much to bring to the table?*

HG—Let me say what student experience is not. It is not a romantic celebration of adolescence as it sometimes was in the sixties. It is something very different. I am arguing that the notion of experience has to be situated within a theory of learning, within a pedagogy. You can't deny that students have experiences, and you can't deny that these experiences are relevant to the learning process even though you might say that these experiences are limited, raw, unfruitful, or whatever. Students have memories, families, religions, feelings, languages, and cultures that give them a distinctive voice. We can critically engage that experience and we can move beyond it. But we can't deny it.

BM—What about the white, middle-class voice?

HG—That's a voice too.

BM—But isn't it more than a voice? Isn't it the model we set? Doesn't is encapsulate the best experiences we want to emulate? To be blunt, isn't the best voice an urban minority student can adopt that of the white middle class?

HG—In an instrumental sense, that is true. But it is a truth that conceals dangers. The problem with that position is that it makes it hard for people to realize how important the question of voice is. We become unquestioning and fail to realize the symbolic violence the dominant voice can exercise. And I will say this: Even for the white, middle-class majority, education often—most often—functions to silence rather than empower them.

BM—A telling point. You make teaching sound like very hard work.

HG—It is very hard work. That is why teachers need to be intellectuals, to realize that teaching is a form of mediation between different persons and different groups of persons, and we can't be good mediators unless we are aware of what the referents of the mediation we engage in are. Teaching is complex, much more complex than mastering a body of knowledge and implementing curricula. The thing about teaching is that the specificity of the context is always central. We can't get away with invoking rules and precedures that cut across contexts.

BM—Your view of education seems to make tradition irrelevant.

HG—As I mentioned before, the nature of our educational problems is new and unprecedented. In that sense, there is no tradition to appeal to. But there are elements of a critical pedagogy in all traditions. The radical educator deals with tradition like anything else. It must be engaged and not simply received. Traditions are important. They contain great insights, for understanding both what we want to be and what we don't want to be. The question is, In what context do we want to judge tradition? Around what sense of purpose? We need a referent to do that. If we don't have a referent, we have no context to make sense of tradition. It doesn't supply its own referent.

BM—Your referent is probably clear by now, but could you state it briefly again?

HG—My referent is, How do we make this country a real critical democracy?

BM—Where do you stand on liberal arts education?

HG—A lot of people think everyone should have a liberal arts education. I disagree with that vehemently. Schooling has its own context. Often that context generates methods of inquiry that aren't likely to surface in the liberal arts disciplines.

BM—You have a new book coming out. What is that about?

HG—It's called *Schooling and the Struggle for Public Life: Critical Pedagogy in the Modern Age.* It will be published by the University of Minnesota Press in the fall of 1988. It is different from my other books in a number of ways. I attempt to redefine the relationship between schooling and democracy, and I look at particular traditions to contextualize this effort. I look at the social reconstructionists of the 1920s, I look at certain traditions in the feminist movement, and I look at some liberation theologians and their sense of struggle and hope. Hope is very important. We have to be able to dream. I also spend a lot of time developing a radical provisional ethic, which is to say an ethic that steers a course between a transcendent, ahistorical referent and a relativity which does not permit an ethic to defend its own presuppositions. Radical educators in this country are capable of a lot of moral indignation but really don't know how to define and justify in an ethical language what they want to do—the particular forms of authority they might want to exercise, the particular programmatic innovations they want to bring about, or, to take on the largest ethical issue of all: What is the nature of the good life we want to defend, and how do we do that in ethical terms? We can't always operate in the logic of resistance. We must be able to speak the language of possibility as well. I chart out the theoretical basis of such an ethic in this book. Another thing I do is talk a lot about student voices. I think the primacy of student experience is crucial. But I have already talked about that.

BM—Can you, as the clock winds down, summarize your educational philosophy?

HG—Probably not, but I'll try. I find myself frequently falling back on a distinction John Dewey made over 40 years ago between "education as a function of society" and "society as a function of education." In other words, are schools to uncritically serve and reproduce the existing society or challenge the social order to develop and advance its democratic imperatives? Obviously, I opt for the latter. I believe schools are the major institutions for educating students for public life. More specifically, I believe that schools should function to provide students with the knowledge, character, and moral vision that build civic courage.

BM—The expression "civic courage" has a nice ring to it.

HG—We are going to need a lot of it.

BM—We'll talk again sometime.

HG—I hope we do.   □

An Interview with
RALPH KETCHAM on
The Problem of Citzenship Education

THE most important conversation going on today, both in this country and in the world generally, is about the meaning of democracy. We seem to have come to one of those watersheds in history when our basic concepts stand in need of redefinition, our political concepts among them. Ralph Ketcham, of Syracuse University, is a vigorous participant in this debate.

The parameters of the conversation may be sketched in the image of a triangle. On one point, we have an understanding of democracy that flows from its classical formulation. Democracy began in Greece as a response to problems that arose when states were ruled by oligarchies. The principal problem it sought to address was the arbitrary rule by self-serving elites or dictators. The remedies proposed included public deliberation to establish power, elections to select leaders, the diffusion of power, and the rule of law. Since, in its original iteration, democracy was direct, participation was a duty. Citizens had a high moral stake in their political community; they believed the polis was the premier means of achieving the good life, of maximally realizing human potential.

With the birth of modern democracy in the seventeenth and eighteenth centuries (what we now refer to as liberal democracy) the focus of political values shifted from the political community to the individual. What liberal democracy means to us today is that government is legitimized by the will of the people, and its principal function is to protect the rights which inhere in each individual naturally. The Declaration of Independence stands as a noble testament to that ideal. With the hindsight of our twentieth-century experience, however, the liberal notion of democracy is widely criticized because it has led, directly or indirectly, to intolerable social pathologies. It is charged that liberalism glorifies individual rights—often reduced to selfish rights—at the expense of common values, leads to egregious inequalities in the social order, and gives an inadequate account of our social nature. Liberal democracy, we frequently hear, has no conception of community.

Socialism is a political response to the defects of liberal democracy. Socialism has taken different forms—the conservative socialism of those who cling to tradition and the supposed holistic values of a Golden Age; Christian socialism, which arose in Europe towards the middle of the nineteenth century to protest the excesses of the Industrial Revolution and shore up an eroding Christian faith; state socialism of the sort we find in communism; and, more recently, welfare socialism, which we associate with the mixed economies of Western European countries. Socialism in all of its expressions emphasizes community, equality, and increasingly, as its history has unfolded in the twentieth century, the authority of the state as the means of realizing these values. In socialism, the community rather than the individual is the primary bearer of rights; the individual is subordinated to the social whole. Socialism runs into trouble when it appeals to authority to enforce its ideal of community and equality. At its worst, this leads to totalitarianism and the repression of political rights. Thus, through many cold wars, liberal democracy and socialism have battled to a standstill.

Now there is a new argument on the block, which attempts to salvage the best of liberalism and socialism and overcome the defects of each. It as yet lacks a name, but it is sometimes referred to as the communitarian option. Ralph Ketcham is a prominent spokesman for this point of view. Ketcham teaches American studies and is an authority on the Founding Fathers. He has written widely on early American political thought and most recently published *Individualism and American Life,* which is a major statement of what I have referred to as the communitarian option. Ketcham seeks a middle ground between the excessive individualism of the liberal tradition and the excessive authoritarianism of the socialist tradition. He seeks to make room for community, traditions, civic virtue, social practices, and the public interest. Ketcham has made a fresh contribution to what it means to be a citizen in a democratic society and how education may serve that aim. The following interview reflects the best of Ketcham's thinking.

BM—Everyone agrees that there is a problem with citizenship in America. How do you see that problem?

RK—For the past 20 to 30 years, it has been a problem of neglect. For example, college catalogues everywhere extol the virtues of citizenship, but not much is done to fulfill those claims.

BM—But it must be deeper than mere neglect.

RK—Yes, it is. I think the basic philosophical reason is the excessive individualism of the Western tradition, its lack of a robust sense of community.

BM—Surely the Western tradition has a sense of community.

RK—It does. But the Judeo-Christian tradition at a fundamental level emphasizes the relationship of the individual to God, and this gives the individual a claim over against the state and other communities with the overall effect that it infantilizes the political, the here and now. It doesn't want to take the city of man too seriously. The latest version of that attitude is Reagan's campaign to get government off our backs. It's amazing to me that we could think of government as the enemy. So, even though there is good communitarian thinking in the Western tradition, like Aristotle's notion of government as an instrument of the good life, or the civic humanist tradition which affirms that we find our human fulfillment in the polity, it remains true that that is always counterbalanced by the claims of individualism.

BM—What about the thinking of the founders of the American republic?

RK—The founders were transitional thinkers. On the one hand, they thought with the classical philosophers; on the other hand, they were enamored of the newer notions of Locke and Hobbes that elevated the isolated individual. And they didn't regard these poles of their thinking as contradictory. Jefferson was a liberal in the modern sense, but, as well, he read Aristotle and Cicero. In my opinion, what happened is that, as the nineteenth century wore on, the boundary between these two poles became distorted, and eventually the older tradition died out. By the time of Andrew Jackson's administration, party politics was beginning to be validated as it never had before, and about the same time, De Toqueville, who was as far as I know the first thinker to coin the word individualism, was also the first to see it as a problem. By the time we get to social Darwinism, the competitive energies of human nature are emphasized almost exclusively. We have only lately come to see the devastating effects of the liberal revolution that marks the beginning of modern thought.

BM—How does Lincoln fit in here?

RK—Lincoln understood the uses of government. His emphasis was on the union. Lincoln had a good moral sense, pointing out the objections to slavery and the necessity of sacrifices to hold the union together.

BM—Would he be a transitional thinker in the sense you indicated?

RK—I think so. Lincoln is often seen as occupying a kind of middle position between two traditions in American political thought: one that flows from liberal philosophy and social contract theory and the other that flows from the covenantal tradition of the Puritans. Much of Lincoln's moral passion probably was imbibed from that source.

BM—Suppose I were to argue that Americans generally occupy that middle position, that they are, as someone has said, pragmatic idealists. On the one hand, they go to church on Sunday, and, on the other, they get back to making money on Monday.

RK—There is truth in that characterization. And, as I said, in the beginning our leaders had a foot in both camps. My claim is that the tendency has been toward the individualistic pole of that equation, and in the United States since 1945 there has been a disproportionate, and I would even say pathological, emphasis on it. The paradoxes and flaws of postwar American public life reveal a degenerative, self-sustaining cycle of self-interest and public infantilism.

BM—And you lay that to liberal political philosophy?

RK—Yes. In the philosophies of Locke and Hobbes, the assumption is that the individual will is at the center of existence. That assumption sets the stage for conflict-of-interest politics. If, as Locke argues, the purpose of government is the preservation of our "lives, liberties, and estates," then we are predisposed to use the public arena to gain personal advantages and ends. Thus, we teach our children how to make it in such a system, how to calculate their own advantage.

BM—*Describe a better model.*

RK—Plato's *Republic* properly set the question: How can virtue—wisdom, courage, temperance, and justice—essential to the good life, be made the foundation of the state? Plato answers that the state must be ruled by those who embody this virtue. Decisions that guide and mold the shared life of the community must be made according to the standards of virtue. Only then will society go beyond mere survival or material wealth or power to the *good life* itself. Plato thus emphasized the education and training of those who would rule in order to ensure that they will indeed be wise, courageous, temperate, and just. In addition, firm distancing of rulers from the prejudicing temptations of family and ownership of property, and long practice in the efficient, disinterested administration of public affairs are insisted upon to ensure the *quality* of rule required for the good of society as a whole.

BM—*Was this the origin of the civic humanism tradition?*

RK—Yes. From Aristotle, who said that the state can be perfect only when "all have the virtue of the good citizen," through the Christian writers, like Thomas Aquinas and Erasmus, who were interested in the education of the Christian prince, to the Renaissance philosophers, who elaborated in greatest detail the philosophy of civic humanism, is a straight line. And I place Jefferson in that lineage. With him, we see the democratization of the classical heritage; with him and his contemporaries, the people themselves were the source of power.

BM—*Is John Dewey part of that tradition?*

RK—Yes. John Dewey founded a movement for the "progressive" transformation of the public schools in order to better educate for democratic citizenship. He also worked endlessly to reform American political and economic life so that the "collective intelligence of the group," grass-roots groups of common people, might act knowledgeably and constructively on public affairs. In each case, the equation is the same: If human society is to be well, wisely, virtuously governed, then the governors must be wise and virtuous, whether they are one, a few, or many.

BM—*You also draw extensively on traditions of the East.*

RK—Yes. I think I am very lucky to be able to balance my thinking with Oriental thought.

BM—How does that help?

RK—For the Orientals, and I speak primarily of the Confucian tradition, humanity is constituted by relationships. We, as individuals, are defined by actions, loyalties, and responsibilities that are social in nature. Our notion of the autonomous individual is simply appalling to them.

BM—Would you want to say that this ethos has produced a better polity?

RK—That is not the point I am making. I am saying they understand better our social natures—our embeddedness in culture, tradition, history, and nationhood.

BM—But surely it is not a small matter that Confucian thought does not provide for participation by ordinary people in government. It is not democratic.

RK—No, it isn't. Governing is supposed to be done in accordance with a wise elite, from the top down. But even though government is not by the people, it has to be for the people, for their good. That is a very active and provident notion. Government is important and to be taken seriously. That is something we can learn from Eastern thought.

BM—You seem to be saying that we don't take government seriously.

RK—No, we don't

BM—Are you also saying that government is the condition of community?

RK—A necessary but not sufficient condition. Vitality in the private sector is fine. We need voluntarism and associations of all kinds so long as these do not distract us from attending explicity to the affairs of the polity. We kid ourselves if we think collaborative action in the private sector can substitute for it at the public level.

BM—Let's turn to the question of education and the curriculum. As an educator, do you sometimes have a queasy feeling in your stomach?

RK—Oh, yes. We educators are not doing nearly enough to inculcate a sense of citizenship, and schools fall far short of fulfilling their roles as civic institutions. Faculty are largely miseducated in this regard and will probably take a generation or two to get back on track.

BM—Do you think education did a better job earlier?

RK—Yes. As long as there was a fairly intelligible, agreed-upon core, citizenship values were at least implicit in that core. The core in schools was supported by a value consensus in society at large. At least much more of a consensus than we have now.

BM—Do you think the curriculum can do the job it once did?

RK—Well, it can do a lot better than it is doing.

BM—How would you redesign it to accommodate citizenship requirements?

RK—I use the analogy of language. We all have to be competent in the English language. We are also all citizens. This, too, requires explicit attention. I see no objection to a required course in citizenship comparable to freshman English, although we probably wouldn't call it that. Why couldn't we designate part of our distribution requirements in such a way that explicit attention is given to citizenship? Another suggestion I have is to build a citizenship component into professional courses. We haven't given much attention lately to professionals as citizens, to what the Puritans used to refer to as their general calling. Imagine what might happen if our doctors, lawyers, accountants, nurses, merchants, etc., were hit hard with general citizenship requirements!

BM—But wouldn't such courses be subject to all the problems the old civics courses fell prey to?

RK—Not necessarily. They were taught by faculty who weren't particularly interested in them and on a very narrow, flag-waving kind of basis. The courses I propose would be as substantive as any offered in the curriculum and taught by qualified faculty. My proposal is pitched to a much higher intellectual level. It is important to educate for citizenship within a solid intellectual framework.

BM—You seem to be suggesting that there is an academic solution to the problem of citzenship, and a curriculum-intensive solution at that. Where does the experiential come in?

RK—I don't think we can substitute the experiential for the academic, but I don't think we can do without it either. Both are necessary. If I were to come up with some kind of formula for citizenship education, it would have three parts: one part conviction, one part understanding, and one part virtue.

BM—Say something about each part. What do you mean by conviction?

RK—We all have to be convinced that we all participate in government, even if only by not noticing, not speaking, or not acting, thus allowing others to discern and decide public issues. The only office we all are sure to fill is that of citizen, an office which, as much as any vocation or role, may require careful preparation for its proper fulfillment. The essence of the office is not exceptional intelligence, or a mass of knowledge, or high skill in research and analysis, or an intricate understanding of the process of government, or even the habit of involvement in politics—though all of these things are desirable and useful. Rather, fundamentally, a citizen must have in some degree the perspective of interest in the society as a whole, not a narrower individual or group point of view. Though each person in a free society properly has private rights or goals, in a free, *self-governing* community each person also holds the *public* office of citizen. When acting in that capacity the citizen must have as much as possible the disinterested, judicious, wise qualities always admired in good rulers. The office of citizen requires, then, that its holders be interested in public and private concerns. This conviction must undergird all civic education and all participation in self-government.

BM—*And the understanding part?*

RK—That means a grasp of the philosophy of the civic arts tradition. What we were talking about a moment ago.

BM—*Mortimer Adler once said that the only two things we have in common are that we are all citizens and that we are all philosophers, by which he meant that we have to think about what it means to be a citizen. You seem to be saying something similar.*

RK—Basically, yes.

BM—*What about the virtue part of the formula?*

RK—Here I am talking about civic virtue. The need is not that citizens necessarily devote large amounts of time to public concerns or that they be "experts" in all the details of government, but rather that they ask the proper *public* question, "What is good for society as a whole?" not the corrupt private one, "What public policy will suit my personal, special needs?" Citizens must bring an attitude formed by words like "obligation," "responsibility," and even "duty" to their public role, rather than a perspective formed by words like "desire," "drive," and "interest." The public and civic virtue required of the responsible citizen is, after all, a moral quality. The civic model of citizenship does not deny human self-interestedness, but a person becomes a *responsible* citizen in so far as he or she, through education, moral instruction, occupational influence, political practice, and conscientious resolve, is able to curb selfish tendencies and instead achieve some degree of public perspective. There is no expectation that the selfish drive can be entirely eliminated or that the public perspective can be completely attained. The belief, though, is that ability to achieve a public perspective is in some degree present in human nature, and that steady effort by human beings in society *can* yield enough public spiritedness to make government by the people in some degree *good* government. The idea is not that people will soon or easily discard long-held habits of self-centered citizenship, but that a change in the concept of participation (begun with change in the attitudes as young people learn about citizenship) can gradually alter the quality of public life.

BM—How did you become interested in the question of citizenship education?

RK—I sort of grew into it. In high school, I was a current events junkie. In college, I got trapped for some committee work, but I wasn't really an activist. In time, I came to major in history and political science, and eventually to teach those subjects. In that way, my interest grew, whetted, of course, by all the disturbing problems in contemporary society.

BM—I assume you are calling for such curricular implementation at all levels of education?

RK—Absolutely. From kindergarten though the Ph.D. programs. As a matter of fact, I have recently collaborated on writing a textbook for a requirement in the New York state school system. Now every high school senior must take a course in citizenship.

BM—This and other initiatives would seem to indicate that interest in citzenship education is reviving. Would you agree?

RK—I think that is the case.

BM—What are some of the reasons for this?

RK—Well, I think the basic reason is the perception that our polity isn't working very well. We are not generating the kinds of leaders, the kinds of policy responses, or the kind of public awareness that would, so to speak, do us justice. If we ask why the polity isn't working very well we have to answer with Pogo that "we have met the enemy and he is us." The people themselves lack training and perspective in exercising the office of citizenship. In a democracy, this can only lead to bad results.

BM—Are there some other reasons?

RK—I think an important one is the increasing, interdependent nature of our world. There are many nagging questions about the quality of life that worry people. Take the environmental problems. Here, the notion of a public interest is clear. There is an agreement on this. We may not know what to do with hazardous waste, but we at least agree it is a hazard and that we have to begin to think about this problem. Issues like that generate public spirit and a sense of community.

BM—That word "community" is troublesome. For some, it conjures up images of totalitarian forms of government, so any appeal to community has a built-in scare factor. Is that a problem for you?

RK—What you say is true. People tend to think of conformity and the subjection of the individual to the whole. But I am simply unwilling to let the totalitarians take the word community away from us or take the notion of effective government away from us.

BM—Would you agree that the Declaration of Independence is our best civic document because it speaks a more communitarian language?

RK—I would have no problem with that. But I would also want to say that the Constitution is a fulfillment of the Declaration. There were varying opinions on this at the time of the Constitutional Convention, but in my view, both the Federalists and anti-Federalists were faithful to the spirit of the Declaration.

BM—Why can't the Declaration and the Constitution serve as the basic texts for citizenship education? Why do we have to look further?

RK—That would suit me fine, provided we add some key Supreme Court cases to show how the Constitution can be given meaning in later periods. I would be perfectly happy to rest the case for citizenship education in this manner.

BM—Then why don't we do it? The answer is staring us in the face.

RK—The difficulties are practical ones. Someone is sure to hop up and say the Constitution validated slavery and doesn't include women.

BM—There are the Amendments.

RK—They help. But that doesn't meet the argument that the Constitution itself was deficient.

BM—But you don't think it was deficient?

RK—I don't think it was perfect. But it was adequate to the circumstances, and it has served us well, and serves especially as a basis for developing a democratic polity that is sustained by public spiritedness and an active citizenry who are skilled in the habits of discussion and decision making.

BM—How would you rate American democracy today?

RK—Fairly low. It is not dead. But something is clearly wacky when we set the people against the government. We have wonderful traditions, a good Constitution, and the experience of over 200 years of self-government. These are positive legacies, and we are living off that capital. So far we've gotten by. The question is: Can we continue to do so?   □

An Interview with
CHRISTOPHER LASCH on

The Social Role
of the Educator

THE substance of this interview appeared in the first issue of *The Antaeus Report* in the fall of 1980. Christopher Lasch had just published his best-seller *The Culture of Narcissism*, which remains the classic critique of the "me" generation. In it, he had some hard-hitting things to say about the state of higher learning in America. He wrote, for example: "Not only does higher education destroy the students' minds; it incapacitates them emotionally as well, rendering them incapable of confronting experience without benefit of text-books, grades, and pre-digested points of view." He also wrote: "The university remains a diffuse, shapeless, and permissive institution that has absorbed the major currents of cultural modernism and reduced them to a watery blend, a mind-emptying ideology of cultural revolution, personal fulfillment, and creative alienation."

Strong words! In fact, at the time, I thought them excessive. But what I understood from the interview was that Lasch's criticisms of higher education were part of a broader analysis of our political culture. The disintegration of our public life was the focus of his concerns. That was in the book, of course. He spoke there quite eloquently of our eroding liberties, the new paternalism of government, the Midgard-like grip of huge bureaucracies, and the substitution of therapeutic justice for retributive justice. In fact, he came down hard in his book on the professions for their lack of civic concern. They, too, have become engulfed in the pursuit of narcissism. Some of Lasch's recent writings have contributed significantly to the literature, pointing a way out of our public philosophy impasse. He argues that our choices historically have been limited to some form of liberalism, on the one hand, and some form of collectivism on the other. Each has led to unacceptable social pathologies. Liberalism has emphasized individual rights and autonomy to the great detriment of community and the common good. Collectivism has gone in the other direction and usually ended in authoritarian regimes and political repression. Lasch now talks about the communitarian compromise as a middle position. What we need, he says, is a political conception of community that can overcome the excesses of liberal individualism and the coying, holistic conception of community that ends in a sentimental glorification of the past. Social solidarity, he wrote in a recent article, "does not rest on shared values or ideological consensus, let alone on an identity of interests; it rests on public conversation." That is an insight that opens rich perspectives on our contemporary debates and indicates a role for education that we have not seriously contemplated in the recent past.

BM— You write on a wide range of subjects. Do you see yourself as a historian, a social critic, a philosopher at large, a man of letters, or what?

CL—I am a historian by training and am comfortable with the designation cultural historian.

BM—You have been a sharp critic of academia. Do you find academia conducive to the kind of writing you do?

CL—Yes and no. Academia offers a good deal of personal freedom. I don't experience any immediate restraints. But, obviously, it isn't the kind of environment that is going to generate much critical thought.

BM—There's an irony!

CL—That's for sure.

BM—Where is a better place? You're not likely to see critical thought coming from the media or political parties. How about think tanks and such para-academic institutions?

CL—They're even worse.

BM—Even worse?

CL—Yes. They are even more integrated into the power system. After all, they exist directly to service it. When students protested the kind of military research done on campuses, they didn't reckon the consequences of their demand: It would go into high-level think tanks where scholars are freed of the kind of checks and balances we find in universities, without even vestigial responsibilities toward students. There is something deadly about the high-level discussions of "values" that take place in think tanks. The discussion is premised on some kind of assumption that is guaranteed to make it marginal, to make sure that values, no matter how earnestly they are discussed, never impinge on action.

BM—In a Change *article some years ago, you claimed that education conceived as meritocracy is discriminatory and a degeneration of the democratic ideal. Do you still hold to that thesis?*

CL—I haven't seen anything to change my mind. What has happened is that the whole educational system has increasingly been pressed into the needs of industry. It comes to serve as a device to select manpower. Every other objective is necessarily subordinated to that. This is particularly true in the lower educational system, but the university has been shaped by the same kinds of needs.

BM—Would you make distinctions between different kinds of universities in this respect?

CL—The difference, I think, is that different schools exist to train different kinds of manpower. Some exist to train a political and managerial elite, others for middle-level bureaucratic jobs, etc. The system, thank God, doesn't operate as efficiently as it was intended to. Its growth was to some extent haphazard, and many traditional elements co-exist alongside the career emphasis. There have always been contending views of how the university ought to be organized. In the end, none of them quite established its ascendancy. The most powerful forces, however, have been those who wanted to make the university a high-class service institution. The fact that there have been contending and contradictory voices is one of the reasons why the university is such a muddle today.

BM—Still, I wonder if meritocracy is quite the right word here. Merit would seem to imply something more than just training manpower for the market. The word makes one think of accomplishment, excellence, achievement, and the like.

CL—Well, there is a paradox here. Neither our society nor our educational system is really based on achievement. The general aim is to blend in, mix, and be well-liked. We can see that in our emphasis on sports. What on the surface looks like achievement often turns out to be just another way of conforming, of peer approval or celebrity.

BM—Celebrity is a form of conformity?

CL—Oh, yes. Celebrities more than anybody embody the mass values of our society. The minute they don't, they cease to be celebrities.

BM—An interesting idea. But back to the meritocracy question. Could you clarify that further?

CL—I think the confusion is between merit and credentialing. What our educational system measures is not so much achievement as the determination and capacity to stay in school for many years, thereby acquiring the academic certification deemed indispensable for the workplace. We know there is not much correlation between skills taught in school and skills required in the workplace. Nonetheless, we persist in the belief that a long period of schooling is required for social and economic advancement.

BM—But if all we are doing is credentialing, that doesn't seem a sufficient condition for social success.

CL—It is when we consider how it works in practice. When we examine the matter carefully, we note two things: It is usually those who are already well placed in the social system who get most of the credentialing. So there is already in place a network of connections with the right people. Our society is one in which economic success is largely "fixed" (like prices). It results from negotiations with those who can arrange things for us: jobs, tax favors, important contracts, legal services, and so forth. Looked at in this way, favoritism—not merit and certainly not educational merit—is the secret of success in America.

BM—Your mind seems to move in a dialectical fashion. You have written of how modern culture can be seen in terms of a chain of substitute values. For example, enlightened self-interest has given way to an emphasis on the irrational motives of human conduct; sin has been replaced by sickness; punishment by treatment; and so forth. What would you say is now substituted for learning?

CL—I think we could say social control. We have an educational system which has been molded pretty deliberately for selection, rationalization, and control.

BM—The paradox here seems to be that liberal education has become illiberal education.

CL—To a large degree that is true.

BM—This seems to be an indication of a semantic confusion that we notice right across the spectrum. For example, in the political arena, the traditional vocabulary now tends to mean something different. Terms like liberal, conservative, socialist, radical, and the like, are all kind of blending into one another. Conservatives call themselves the true liberals. Liberals stand for socialist and radical causes. It is striking, for example, that in much social criticism radicals are often aligned with conservative positions, especially in their critique of education. Do you see yourself as in some sense a conservative or at least supporting conservative points of view?

CL—I am very much aware of these semantic confusions. I realize, too, that some of the arguments I put forth can be very easily put to conservative purposes. Bear in mind that many conservatives or neoconservatives were once radicals or at least left of center, as many of the *Commentary* people were during the fifties and sixties. While they have moved away from their former positions, they still retain some of their former sentiments and to some extent their former vocabulary as well. Also, a radical critique of education shares with conservatism a central assumption: To wit, most people are incapable of any sustained intellectual exertion. Therefore, any attempt to uphold standards is elitist. The radical critic, of course, won't go all the way with the conservatives. For example, radicals will argue that minorities should have access to higher education, and if standards have to be lowered to accommodate them, then so be it. The true conservative makes no bones about it. Education is elitist, and that is all there is to it. Of course, I would want to question that assumption.

BM—What can we do to give our vocabularies more specificity and avoid some of the confusions we have just talked about?

CL—As a first step toward clear thinking on this subject, let us try to reconstruct the reasons originally underlying our national faith in education. We have inherited from the nineteenth century an educational system, itself rooted in a much older tradition in Western culture, revived, reinvigorated, and reinterpreted—often misinterpreted as well—first by the Renaissance and later by the republican ideology that shaped our political culture in its formative years. Even in the nineteenth century, the ideas and assumptions on which our educational system was based were already beginning to lose their meaning, because the social and cultural context in which they had originated, and which alone could have made them intelligible, had disappeared. Modern moral utterance and practice, says the philosopher Alasdair MacIntyre, can only be understood as a series of fragmented survivals from an older past. In the tradition of social thought stretching back to antiquity, education is not seen as a means to an end—personal advancement, social control, professional training, or even good citizenship. It is seen as an end in its own right, to which other activities are ancillary. The entire political order, in the ancient view, is an essentially educational enterprise. Its purpose is the training of character. According to the ancients, man is a political animal who requires civic relations for his perfection. Citizenship and politics are means to the good life, which defines itself in contrast to the household, the realm of unfreedom where men are bound to the material necessities of reproduction and subsistence. Public life is the realm of freedom, in the sense that men encounter each other in public as equals, not in the relations of domination and subordination that necessarily characterize the household. The political community unites men in a shared vision of the good. It frees them from biological and material necessity in order that they can submit voluntarily to the discipline of citizenship.

BM—What direction should the reform of education take?

CL—At the lower levels, I think we should go back to basic education. The aim should be defined to provide a good basic training in reading, writing, logic, and math. Drop everything else.

BM—At what point do we begin to form what John Dewey liked to call the social intelligence? Or is that really a job for education?

CL—I don't think it is. I have the impression that education became concerned with forming a social intelligence or a political character or whatever we want to call it after the educational element that was once present in other activities like work had been done away with. Before there was a highly integrated system of mass education, people got an education in all kinds of informal ways: in families, in work experience, etc. When that kind of education became difficult to obtain, the demand arose that experience be imported into the school system and recreated in an academic atmosphere.

BM—That's an interesting point. Santayana once said that the problem with undergraduate education is that it attempts to derive experience from ideas. You are saying there is no substitute for experience.

CL—That's right. Even though I sympathize with Dewey's urge to unite experience with learning and his insistence that learning is not just an intellectual process, I don't think that's a job for the schools. I don't think learning can be a substitute for other kinds of experience that are both more basic and more important.

BM—There is an interesting irony here because modern students have more experience than previous generations. Yet they don't seem to learn from it, or, if they do learn from it, there is some kind of dichotomy between what they learn from experience and what they learn in an academic setting.

CL—What kinds of experiences are you thinking of?

BM—Well, they are subject to such powerful agencies as the media for one thing. They have a variety of life experiences of drugs, travel, and sex. The point is, students don't seem to mature as a result of their greater exposure to experience. Isn't that paradoxical?

CL—I think the reason for this is the kinds of experiences you mention are so often prepackaged. Travel is a good example. In our world, the hazard, uncertainty, and risk of travel have been so reduced that it has lost much of its educative value. Our students do a lot of traveling in the sense that they are often to be found in foreign parts. But they rarely come up against a way of life that is truly different from their own. They skim the experience of other societies. One can go around the world and always stay in a Hilton hotel. You might as well stay home. Experience takes comprehension as well as participation.

BM—What we have then is experience as a series of episodes.

CL—Yes. The kind of experience that deprives students of an opportunity to test their own powers. And education thus becomes yet one more episodic experience, the production of prepackaged experience. We are not convinced that we have an experience unless it is processed and labeled in some way like a course. So we have courses in everything . . . how to live and the like. The curriculum itself is a series of episodes. Take this, take that. All I can say is, first of all, the contribution of formal education is necessarily modest. If we could reach general agreement on this point, then a lot of pressure would be taken off the school system.

BM—This line of analysis seems to raise with greater urgency the question of political formation, of how we are to set about recovering healthy democratic instincts. If social agencies at large have lost their educative potency and the schools fail similarly, then how are we to come by political intelligence? What kind of answer can you give this kind of question?

CL—I would argue that the purpose of higher education, the contribution of higher education to democratic institutions, is critical thinking. But what does it mean when we come down to the concrete questions of curriculum and concrete political questions? That's not easy.

BM—What are the prospects for curriculum reforms?

CL—They will be difficult to implement, and, to the extent they are implemented, they will be diluted. The whole modern university is erected on a compromise which relieves the research-oriented faculty from disagreeable teaching chores. The elective system largely relieves faculty of the need to address a captive audience in their classes. They can expect, in the elite schools anyway, to teach students who have chosen a specialty. A major reason for the present muddle of higher education is that faculty want to do their own work rather than teach or advise or do many of the other tasks that go with teaching. They won't surrender this privilege without a tremendous struggle.

BM—So the faculty themselves are prepackaged and preprogrammed, by virtue of the kind of education they have and the kinds of attitudes this education has shaped, to act in certain predictable ways. What you are saying, then, is that the faculty is going to have to make some committment to teaching.

CL—Yes. Until they do, our already bad situation can only worsen. Unless modern science or any other branch of knowledge can be communicated to the intelligent layman, then we are in grave danger of being controlled by an intellectual elite.

BM—Can we have anything like a core curriculum if we don't have a core society? Society is segmented, and if education reflects society's values and demands, doesn't it follow that higher education is rather powerless to undertake initiatives for its own reform?

CL—But that's the saving thing! Higher education isn't only a mirror of society's values. It also reflects a different set of values which are to some degree autonomous or at least potentially autonomous. The ideal of humane learning is not, so far as I can see, tied to any one socioeconomic system. Add to this our universal sense of dissatisfaction with our students, and I think we have a point of departure for reform.

BM—Might not this dissatisfaction with students be a kind of mask for some radical self-discontent on the part of the faculty—an expression of their unhappiness with what they are doing and the way they have been educated?

CL—I think in part it is.

BM—So we have an element of guilt here. Faculty don't at bottom think they ought to be elitist, specialized, playing the role of the high priest, etc.?

CL—I would tend to locate the guilt in faculty awareness of the hollowness of their professional commitment. Their professional ethos is shaped by forces which they don't officially acknowledge. The way research is financed, for example, inhibits freedom in all sorts of ways. Many can live quite happily with these arrangements, but others have a conscience that hurts them a bit. And this is a good thing, too.

BM—Might not one of the ways to get at this problem be more dialogue on the campus among faculty and especially among the different disciplines?

CL—My experience has been that there is no way to promote that kind of dialogue, except perhaps discussion about curriculum reform and, thus, a rethinking of the whole question of what we should be teaching. The only other way is some political disturbance in society at large. The Vietnam War and student protest generated a lot of discussion. That was the only time colleagues ever talked to one another in a serious way about educational issues. Students were demanding a relevant education. Even though there was a lot of sloganeering then, there were nonetheless basic questions raised.

BM—Would you look to the radical tradition rather than the liberal or conservative tradition for this vocabulary of relevance? We need a language, a kind of lingua franca *to bridge the various splits between academics, between the academy and society, etc.*

CL—What you really mean is we need a whole new political orientation. It is true that our languages and traditions are to some serious extent bankrupt. This includes whatever is meant by the radical tradition. Much of the socialist tradition has to be rethought just as much as any other. I think you are on to something though. It is probably useless to talk about the need for conversation across disciplinary lines. There has been a lot of experimentation in this direction, and it really hasn't come to much. It's going to have to be a political language, ultimately, that permits people to talk to one another. The sixties might have led us to this, but it turned out badly. We are worse off now than we were before, at least as far as education is concerned.

BM—I'm impressed by the way this conversation has shifted from a discussion of education and the curriculum to a discussion of the political conditions of education. I think you are absolutely right when you say that we will have to develop a political language before we can talk to one another. Let me now ask, Do you find anywhere in our society efforts to do that?

CL—There is a very promising debate going on at the present time that may break the deadlock between the right and the left which has grown quite fruitless and which, in fact, has paralyzed some of our best efforts at social reconstruction in the recent past. For want of a better word I call it the communitarian debate. Communitarians are critical of the individualism stressed by the liberals, and they are equally critical of the kind of organic community that conservatives want to bring back.

BM—Who are some of the players in this debate?

CL—In many ways, the most important thinker among them is Alasdair MacIntyre, whose book, *After Virtue* (1981), has provoked a great deal of commentary and criticism. Michael Sandel's *Liberalism and the Limits of Justice* (1982) is another indispensable book. The interested reader should also consult Thomas Spragens' *Irony of Liberal Reason* (1981), Jeffery Stout's *Flight from Authority* (1981), and Michael Waltzer's *Spheres of Justice* (1983), not to mention the exhaustive historical scholarship on civic humanism and republicanism, much of it inspired by J. G. A. Pocock's *The Machiavellian Moment* (1975). Finally, there is the wide-ranging study of individualism by Robert Bellah, Richard Madsen, William Sullivan, Ann Swidler, and Steven Tipton, recently published under the title *Habits of the Heart* (1985). No other book has done so much to bring the communitarian critique of liberalism to general attention.

BM—What is the gist of the debate?

CL—It goes like this. What has been missing in the debate about individualism and community is the possibility of a conversational relationship with the past, one that seeks not to deny the past (as liberalism tends to do) or to achieve an imaginative restoration of the past (as conservatives tend to want) but to enter into a dialogue with the traditions that still shape our view of the world. Instead of merely addressing the historical record, we need to grasp the ways in which it addresses us. This will get us away from the nostalgia of thinking of traditions as based on shared values, ideological consensus, or some other presumed identity of interests. Traditions embody conflict as well as consensus. In many ways, this is what is most important about them.

BM—What do we learn when we learn that traditions embody conflicts?

CL—We learn that social solidarity rests on public conversation. It rests on social and political arrangments that serve to encourage debate instead of foreclosing it, and to encourage debate, moreover, not just about conflicting economic interests but about morality and religion, the ultimate human concerns. Public conversation means the systematic cultivation of the rhetorical arts and of the virtues classically associated with eloquence. It means respect for the power of persuasion, which is quite different from the ability to win every argument. Nothing testifies more clearly to the debasement of contemporary politics than the equation of "rhetoric" with ideological manipulation, electioneering, and hot air. The devaluation of public discourse is a much more alarming development than the decline of ideological consensus. In order to counter it, we need to develop a political conception of the community in place of the organic and sentimental conception that now tends to prevail.

BM—One begins to glimpse some implications for education from this way of looking at the matter.

CL—Yes. One implication, as I just noted, would be to elevate rhetoric and other disciplines that promote good conversation to a place of centrality in the curriculum. And I can mention two others. One is the classical conception of history as the story of great lives. More than a pedagogical device designed to instill patriotic sentiments, this narrative conception of the past retained something of the classical belief that men disclose themselves most fully in public actions; that the meaning of those actions becomes clear only in retrospect, once the story is played out to the end; and that we ourselves gain moral insight into our own lives by vicariously reliving the lives of exemplary heros. But the most important legacy of the classical tradition was the belief, which revealed itself more in educational practice than in theory, that the proper and distinctive business of formal education is the training of judgment or practical reason, a mode of thinking not to be confused either with the expression of private feelings or aesthetic preferences, with the goal-directed thinking known to the ancients as technical reason, or with the claim to universality associated with cognitive reason, science, and speculative philosophy. Judgment belongs to the active life, as opposed to the contemplative life, but it does not just pursue practical results. Judgment is the kind of intellectual skill one learns in the course of training for a practice (like architecture, chess, or the art of political oratory), but it pursues the goods internal to that practice, not the external goods that seem so important to us. Considered from this point of view, the choice of means has to be governed by their conformity to standards of excellence designed to extend human capacities for self-understanding and self-mastery.

BM—You seem to be saying two things here. Our sense of political community determines our concept of education. But, even more importantly, when we understand political community as you explain it, we have to understand education broadly as a function of the workplace and social practices and not just as a function of the schools.

CL—Exactly. What makes it so difficult for us to understand these ideas is the instrumentalization and debasement of practical activity that has occurred in the twentieth century, as a result of which we have almost completely lost sight of the possibility that work and politics can serve as character-forming disciplines. These activities are now understood strictly as means of satisfying material needs. Moral ideas, meanwhile, lose their connection with practical life and with the virtues specific to particular practices, and become confused instead with the exercise of purely personal choices and the expression of personal prejudices and tastes, which can be neither justified nor explained, and which should therefore not be regarded as binding on anyone else. We can now see more clearly, I hope, why the degradation of work and politics has had such a blighting effect on education. By draining both work and politics of their educative content and reducing them to technical activities conducted for the most part by technical experts, this process has not only destroyed the social need for general education, it has also undermined its ideological rationale. It has made the very idea of a general education increasingly incomprehensible. General education makes sense only in the context of a larger conception of the political community, one that has been all but lost. It makes sense only if education is seen as an end in itself, the most important end served not just by the schools but by the political order as a whole. It makes sense only if citizenship is defined as a character-building discipline in its own right, one that demands a great deal of worldly knowledge, a command of language, and a capacity and willingness for debate. This is the quality of mind that a general education ought to encourage; but it is a quality of mind, once again, that has no recognizable social value under the conditions that prevail today, has no meaning at all except in a communal or civic context. The power of discriminating judgment withers very quickly in a society that seeks to replace political debate with instrumental expertise and refers questions of war and peace, for example, to the military; economic questions to the economists; and moral questions, when it thinks of moral questions at all, to specialists in legal ethics, medical ethics, and other ethical technicians.

BM—What is the role of the humanities in promoting this kind of general education?

CL—Humanists make a mistake when they think they are the only ones interested in values. The proper role of humanists is not to bring "human values" to the attention of technicians otherwise engaged in a purely instrumental approach to their calling, but to demand the restoration of the practical or moral element of callings that have degenerated into techniques—to insist, in other words, that moral considerations represent that very essence of practical activity, not another special area of expertise, the claims of which have to be balanced against those of other specialties.

BM—You've given us plenty to think about. We'll end with a couple of quick questions. What's the best recent book on education?

CL—It hasn't been written yet.

BM—What is the most hopeful thing you can say in conclusion?

CL—As I said before, there are various traditions alive and converging in the academy. I don't think we should underestimate the university's potential for a creative contribution. It remains, I believe, the freest of society's institutions. We ought to keep this in mind even though we are going through a dry spell at the moment.

BM—We'll leave it at that. Thank you very much. □

An Interview with
ELIZABETH MINNICH on
The Thinking Citizen

THE first time I met Elizabeth Minnich, we got into one of those heated arguments about political imagination, or some such subject, which no one ever wins but which tend to be intellectually stimulating. I was not only intellectually stimulated but drew from the encounter a pragmatic benefit as well. She agreed to be interviewed for this book. Our first take, at the Kettering offices in Dayton, Ohio, got us off to a good start. The interview continued at her home in Charlotte, North Carolina (which, she takes delight in pointing out, is very near South Carolina), and over several phone calls after that. If I were to editorialize, I would say that it is among the best in this collection.

Minnich has had a varied career. She received her B.A. at Sarah Lawrence College in 1965 and her Ph.D. at the New School for Social Research. She has been Director of Studies and founder of the Continuing Education Program at Hollins College, Assistant to the President and then Associate Dean of the Faculty at Barnard College, and Dean of the Union Graduate School for Experimenting Colleges and Universities, where she is presently a faculty member. She has recived many grants (notably a Fulbright to study and teach in India); consulted and lectured widely ("On over fifty campuses," she told me); written some path-breaking studies, principally on feminism and education; serves as an associate editor of *Signs*; and writes a regular column for the *Charlotte Observer* on issues of public concern.

At New School, Minnich studied with Hannah Arendt, for whom she was also a teaching assistant. This fascinated me, because I regard Arendt as the best social philosopher of the twentieth century, or certainly one of the best. Arendt died in 1975, and I never had the privilege of meeting her, although I came close once when she was teaching at the University of Chicago. Had it not been for the accident of one of those winter storms that swirls in suddenly off Lake Michigan and shuts down airports for miles around, I might have succeeded. Her *Human Condition* is a classic, and her book *On Revolution* is not far behind. Arendt is perhaps best known to the larger public for her work on totalitarianism and her reporting on the Eichmann trial for the *New Yorker*.

I began the interview with a question about Arendt.

BM—What was it like studying with Hannah Arendt?
EM—Exciting would be to put it mildly.
BM—How did you come to study with her?
EM—I'll have to back up a bit. As an undergraduate at Sarah Lawrence, my studies were eclectic but tended toward things like anthropology. One day one of my teachers said that I asked good philosophical questions. I didn't know what that meant exactly, but I took it as a compliment. And I was glad to know there was a term for what I liked to do. I started graduate school at Berkeley in political science, but I didn't find that very satisfying so I went back to New York and applied to the Committee on Social Thought at the University of Chicago. While I was waiting to hear from them, I taught a course at the New School College.
BM—What did you teach?
EM—Well, believe it or not, I taught a real course in the liberal arts.
BM—A real course?
EM—Yes. I taught dialectic, rhetoric, and grammar. The great paradox about our liberal arts colleges is that they do not offer the traditional liberal arts. They offer an array of disciplines, distinguished from each other in fact as in name by subject matter, not the thinking art each develops. We do not teach the trivium of grammar,

logic, and rhetoric, which are in fact as in name modes of thought. Insofar as these get taught at all, it is as part of some other discipline. Logic, for example, tends to get absorbed by philosophy. Today we teach mostly subject matters with the odd outcome that most of our students never learn to think. They mostly memorize. An education that does not emphasize thinking but rather systems of knowledge and information produces scholars who can converse with each other but not with others. They have been prepared to study others as objects.

BM—I take it that philosophy is not just another subject matter.

EM—Not for me, it isn't. Philosophy is about thinking. Anyway, to get back to my story, while I was at the New School, Hannah Arendt came there to teach. That was in 1968. She was by then quite famous, and I had read *The Human Condition.* At some point, I decided to make good use of my time and take a course with her. I was told that I didn't qualify because I wasn't enrolled as a student. So I enrolled. Then I was told that Arendt would only take the 12 most advanced students, and again I didn't qualify. Arendt, however, decided to select the class on the basis of interviews, so I went for an interview.

BM—That must have been scary.

EM—Very. The fact is, I remember very little of it because I was so terrified. When she accepted me, I had no idea why. I couldn't remember how I might have impressed her. But I got an A+ on my first paper and that made me feel better.

BM—What was the paper on?

EM—I analyzed some books on the purge trials, trying to bring out the tension between political power and ideology. I asked questions like "How do thinking people react to ideology?" "What kinds of ideology paralyze thought?" It was all pretty heady stuff.

BM—What was the course?

EM—It was called Political Experience in the Twentieth Century.

BM—Describe that.

EM—It was very unorthodox. Arendt drew up a reading list of novels, plays, history (not much philosophy, oddly enough), and political theory from just before World War I to just after World War II. She was basically interested in what happened to European culture between the two World Wars. The focus wasn't primarily on Nazism, although obviously that was part of it. She was interested in the shift in meaning structures, in what happens to individuals in times of crisis, in why so many people welcomed World War I as a relief. This was a different analysis of political culture, and I was absolutely enthralled with it.

BM—What was Arendt's teaching style like?

EM—She was a lecturer trying not be a lecturer. She asked a lot of questions, but the questions were not to stimulate thinking so much as to recall the text. I always felt they weren't the kinds of questions she really wanted to ask, that she felt bound by her training in the German tradition.

BM—Would you say she was a good teacher?

EM—Yes, but frightening to an American student, largely because she had such demands and was rather abrupt in manner. But she was inspiring as well. What fascinated me was that this could be philosophy. I went on to take several more courses with her. I loved her pluralistic selection of texts and the way she used the texts to engage a conversation with her students. Eventually she became freer in this method, so the conversation was not so much submission to a text as it was an inquiry.

BM—Did Arendt leave a legacy?

EM—She certainly didn't found a school. And she hasn't influenced academics very much, but she is widely read outside of academe and has had an influence on public policy.

BM—Who reads her?

EM—She is read in the most astonishing places—in community organizations, journalism, feminist scholarship, think tanks, places like that.

BM—My impression is that she is beginning to be more read in academia. We have had some critical studies of her work, her books are assigned in different kinds of courses, seminars are given on her thought. I'd say a small cottage industry is developing.

EM—You probably know more about that than I do.

BM—Was she a feminist?

EM—I would say so, although the term wasn't as much used then as it is now.

BM—More on that subject later. Did you do your dissertation on Arendt?

EM—No, I wrote on John Dewey.

BM—How did you get from Arendt to Dewey?

EM—She once said to me that Americans should study their own philosophers. That struck me as odd at the time, but I later realized that Americans tend to breath their culture rather than study it. After New School, I spent a year in India on a Fulbright and realized that there was a lot I didn't know about my own culture.

BM—What aspect of Dewey did you work on?

EM—His political work, including his journalism. Did you know he wrote some 500 articles for the *New Republic* alone? I was interested in Dewey as a publicly engaged philosopher and was fascinated by how he could move from intense theory to complete engagement with the issues of the day. That appealed to me very much.

BM—Have you ever published any of your Dewey work?

EM—No. I've been sitting on it all these years.

BM—You should publish it.

EM—I'm thinking about it.

BM—What is the informing question of Dewey's political philosophy?

EM—The recurring question in his work is: Can there be a philosophy that supports rather than subverts democracy?

BM—Is Dewey our best philosopher of democracy?

EM—I think so. He holds up very well. He was a little naive about the promise of scientific method. But if we read past that to his transactional notion of experience and his naturalistic epistemology, we strike something very rich. I go back to him very often.

BM—Why do you think Dewey has fallen into eclipse?

EM—One answer is that philosophy has become very professional and very narrow. The publicly engaged philosopher of the type he was is not now an esteemed model. He had a freedom to cross boundaries that we don't. At about the time he died in 1952, there was a real struggle for the definition of America going on. We came out of the fifties with what was fundamentally a re-definition. And radical democrats like Dewey lost out.

BM—What was the re-definition?

EM—That's pretty big.

BM—Give it a shot.

EM—I see it this way. Until sometime after World War II, the major belief strand of this country was that republican virtue resided in individuals, in the small businessperson, in the community, in the neighborhood, and in the multiplying of factions. There was an inordinate suspicion of bigness, whether in business or government. Life since then has taken on a more national and corporate character.

Bigness is in, and the tradition of republican virtue was powerfully subverted.

BM—Give me a minute to digest that, then we'll come back to it. Meanwhile, tell us something about what you are doing now. Begin by telling us what the Union Graduate School is.

EM—It was originally called the Graduate School of the Union of Experimenting Colleges and Universities. It is based on an educational model genuinely appropriate for adults who are already for the most part professionals. Our students are distinguished by the fact that they are equals, citizens, responsible, and experienced. So we have broken with the old hierarchical model and offer a genuine alternative. We are not educating people to be "a" something. We are not discipline-defined but interdisciplinary and issue-centered. The main reason why students come to us is that they want to think about something. And the tutorial is the usual mode of teaching.

BM—What do you like best about this kind of teaching?

EM—I am almost never in a position of telling students something and not knowing what they are making of it. Lots of main-line professors lecture for a lifetime without ever knowing that. I can't think of anything more devastating to thinking. Mind you, I don't want to appear anti-lecture. A lecture can be a fine demonstration of public thinking. When Arendt lectured, you were made palpably aware of what thinking is. But it isn't often the case in undergraduate schools. My job is not to say, "This is what you need to know to become a something and these are the prevailing theories." I don't give courses in that sense. My job is to work with students to determine what they want to think about.

BM—What are some of the things your students are thinking about?

EM—Nuclear issues, war and peace, public-policy thinking, the uses of language and forms of discourse, ethical questions of all sorts, the environment, psychological topics. I have one student who is working on nutrition and psychology. That is fairly typical in that it is an attempt to combine things that are separated in conventional graduate programs.

BM—How many students do you have?

EM—Twenty-five would be an average.

BM—Where do you meet them?

EM—It could be anywhere. Their place. My place. Motels. High schools. Wherever. We don't spend money on buildings, but we tend to spend a lot on plane fares.

BM—It sounds highly unstructured.

EM—Yes and no. It is probably not as unorganized as I am making it sound. To begin with, each student works not only with a principal professor but with a committee of six which screens the student in the first place. So there is good supervision. I think of it as a high level, multi-faceted tutorial system.

BM—It certainly seems that what you do is highly congruent with your own philosophy.

EM—It is, and it is an enormous luxury. At issue in both cases is thinking. I carry always the conviction that knowing has social consequences. In other words, epistemology is political. If that is the case, then establishing the relationship between the world and the self, between the self and self, between the self and others defines our sense of what is and what is possible. It defines our understanding of basic values like agency and freedom. If that is the case, then education is at the center of the political and philosophical enterprise, because when we talk about education, we are talking about how individuals relate to reality and to values. Which is to say, we are talking about what people know and the knowing of what they know. This form of knowing is an enactment and a release of agency, of connection, of passion. It is what I think philosophy does and should do. It makes possible the kinds of interesting things that go on between people and their sense of reality. What are we seeing? What are we hearing? How are we engaging? What sense are we making of it? How do things hang together? What is the big picture? Questions like these make of education an intense existential struggle.

BM—What is the role of the teacher?

EM—The teacher is responsible for the process and not only the content. That is the art of teaching. It is a profoundly political art, and I love it.

BM—You must love Socrates then.

EM—I love Socrates.

BM—Was Arendt that kind of teacher?

EM—Not in the practice, at least not most of the time. She was too much in the Germanic mold. But her thinking was. One of the reasons she didn't found a school is because it was always very difficult to say just what her position on any given point was because she was always thinking about it. The effect of listening to her was to have your own thinking affected. To hear her lecture was to practice a kind of thinking with her as she engaged in conversation with Hegel or Kant or whomever. And it was a quite irreverent conversation, I might add, because she considered herself an equal in the conversation. The fact that students were only witnesses to that conversation in no way detracted from its powerful and dramatic impact. It was wonderful teaching.

BM—Let's come down from these empyrean heights for a moment to talk about things as they are. Are you hopeful about our many attempts at educational reform?

EM—What I emphasize in my own work on education is that we live in a radically new age. I want to focus on what is new and then ask how education ought to respond. Education is always a mediator between the past and the future. Some get riveted by the past. Others succumb to the lure of the future. What I am asking is that we hold still for a moment and concentrate on the present so that the mediating function of education can become more thoughtful.

BM—What is the newness of the present?

EM—Let's look at the changing demographics. Many of our students are now non-Western, for whom the dominant Western paradigm is not applicable; many of our students are adults, and they require a different kind of education; and now women are for the first time a presence in education. About eight years ago, women became 51 percent of the undergraduate population. Set this against the history of exclusion in the dominant tradition, and we realize that culture has changed in some radical way. Much more radical than we have been willing to deal with.

BM—How radical?

EM—The fact that there were so many exclusions built into the dominant paradigm leads us to reflect that there were some fundamental conceptual errors built into it. What women's studies have shown is that over half the human race (not just women but lots of men too) were not merely overlooked or ignored, but were systematically excluded. And the exclusion was not accidental, but intentional, deep-rooted, and ideological. It was part of the meaning system, deeply embedded in the language, social structures, the choice of problems, and so forth. I have a nice example which illustrates my point. Some years ago Harry Breverman asked 100 clinical psychologists, psychiatric social workers, and psychologists, both male and female, to describe a "normal" human, a "normal" man, and a "normal" woman. He found that the definitions of "normal" for a man and for a human coincided, while the definition of "normal" for woman differed from both. Thus a woman can be a "normal" woman only if she is an "abnormal" human, and a "normal" human only if she is an "abnormal" woman. What this reveals is that those who were dominant—that is privileged, white males—in the tradition generalized their values for everybody. They set the defining norms, the ideal. Everyone else became a lesser human being, an oddity, an aberration, a sub-text in some way.

BM—Including many men?

EM—Yes, many men. In fact all men lose when only a few men control the paradigm. They have not adequately known, or recognized, or learned about and from the struggles with necessity, the passions of human relations that they have relegated to those who served them. They have known competition, but not the mutual struggle it takes for all of us to win.

BM—What do we do with Socrates? Can people like him be rescued from the defective paradigm?

EM—Socrates was honest enough to credit women from whom he learned, and proudly compared himself to an ignoble midwife when he spoke of how he drew forth ideas from people who claimed to know, assisting not only in the birth but in the often unfavorable evaluation of the product. Imagine how the tradition would have been different had the influence of Socrates and Diotima prevailed rather than that of Aristotle, who argued in a curiously circular way for the natural state of slavery and with suspect biological evidence for the inferiority of women. So I say the move to women's studies is in the Socratic spirit. We, too, put loyalty to truth above loyalty to the tradition, to received knowledge, to those who claim to know, to the presently prevailing packages of kinds of knowing (the disciplines). The cardinal error that Socrates exposed in his questioning was the assumption that one instance can be the type, the ideal, a fundamental error that occurs when too few examples have been considered—as in mistaking the qualities of some few males for human ideals. Like a midwife assisting in a birth who simply brings out what is already there, Socrates drew out the implications of assuming, for example, that justice is simply what is legal. Doing so, he revealed the contradictions inherent in much that we all simply accept. That is what the new scholarship on women does, and it, too, is not always popular.

BM— Can we salvage other thinkers besides Socrates?

EM—Dewey, of course, argued against all dualisms. And Kant was Arendt's favorite philosopher. His ideal of cosmopolitanism was rich. Even old Plato admitted women among his rulers. Actually, I take my philosophical cue from Descartes who performed one of the most interesting thought experiments in all of history when he proposed to doubt everything. Radical doubt to me is a great device. Everything has to be put to the test, but that doesn't mean everything will fail. I don't deny tradition; it's just that we have to be very careful. Some of it is very helpful; some of it is very dangerous. It has to be read with the eye of radical doubt.

BM—Tradition is not the enemy, but the reification of tradition is. Is that what you are saying?

EM—My position is actually twofold. There is a dominant tradition which we have to understand, and to understand profoundly, for good or for ill. And within that tradition there are powerful tools of thought and great oppositional thinkers who thought beyond the limitations of their age and circumstances. It would be foolish to throw that out.

BM—Would you say women's studies are the most exciting part of the curriculum now?

EM—More generally, I would want to say that far and away the most creative educational thinking and practice today is going on in the special studies programs, which include women's studies but also include ethnic studies, peace studies, environmental studies, etc. In these studies, basic assumptions that underlie and shape education elsewhere are brought out and thought through. This happens because special studies must locate and free themselves from that which has made the majority of the population and its most pressing concerns "special" rather than central.

BM—More specifically, how would you assess the status of women's studies?

EM—When we look at any particular campus, we see progress, but only a minority effort. But the aggregrate of what is being done on all campuses and what has been achieved in a relatively short time is stunning. It constitutes a veritable conceptual revolution.

BM—To what do you attribute this progress?

EM—A fascinating question, and there is no one answer to it. For one thing, women were in place. They were always there on the faculty and in the administration, and they brought the scholarship in. Too, it became a social issue like civil rights, and there was an extraordinary burst of energy and organization released by the new questions posed. And we can't forget the preparatory work done by educational theorists like John Dewey and Paulo Freire.

BM—What do you think the signal contributions of women's studies are?

EM—Better thinking. They cracked open questions that had long been thought settled. Women's studies force us to make connections with lived experience, with politics, with the family and society in ways that were not done before. The basic message is: stop and think. The categories you have been using may not be adequate. Think again about justice, about history, about reflexivity, about experience. Perhaps the greatest contribution is to have changed the paradigm. It is no trivial thing when a culture, which for two millennia has an invidious hierarchy of kinds of human beings, in a short space of time changes. That means we are in a genuinely radical new age. Our notions of what it means to be human are altered, so it follows that our notions of what it means to educate and be educated must also change.

BM—What else is new about the present?

EM—Technology, obviously. We need to study that more, from communications to nuclear power. Technology has so radically and so quickly penetrated our culture that we haven't yet begun to think well about it.

BM—Hans Jonas, recently retired from the New School, has written as well as anyone I know on the problems of technology. Did you know him?

EM—Jonas was one of my teachers in graduate school, but I have only recently discovered his writings on technology. I am working with his idea of the heuristics of fear.

BM—I don't recall that. What did he mean?

EM—He is suggesting that in order to take as seriously as we must our responsibility, because of the technological power we now dispose of, we need to counterbalance the euphoria of technological mastery by facing the dramatic fears we can appropriately have. Moral imperatives are frequently cast in the form of "Thou Shalt Not." Today we need some new such imperatives with respect to technology.

BM—Interestingly enough, technology and society courses are right up there with feminist studies in the curriculum. In fact, I teach one myself. I find that students are ambiguous about them. On the one hand, they sign up in large numbers; on the other, they don't seem to engage the subject matter very critically. It is as though they were confronted with something too awesome to comprehend.

EM—It may be like the Holocaust in that regard. We study it, but we can't comprehend it. As I see it, most of the challenge to our thinking falls between the collapsed-dominant paradigm, on the one hand, and the explosion of technological knowledge and power, on the other. We are challenged from those two directions.

BM—And it would seem that we don't find much in the one to help us with the other.

EM—The tradition doesn't have much specific to say about technology or other modern problems. But what I look for is help on how to think. And the tradition offers a lot there, great thought experiments that we can imitate with great profit.

BM—Earlier in our conversation you made the claim that the tradition of republican virtue has been powerfully subverted by modernism. I would like to return to that subject now and ask more about that. Specifically, I would like to ask about citizenship education.

EM—The principal responsibility of the citizen is to think.

BM—To think?

EM—To think.

BM—What about acting?

EM—To think in a way that is like acting.

BM—Could you make a fuller statement about that?

EM—To begin with, I stand with mentors like Hannah Arendt and John Dewey. Public philosophers of that ilk have in common certain features. They have a conviction that we as citizens have to think; they think about thinking; their thinking is not architectonic or puzzle-solving, but issue-oriented and takes into account multiplicity, pluralism, change. They are interested in how ideas have impact on the polity. This makes their thinking a form of action, the activity of becoming a citizen.

BM—Can it be taught?

EM—It can be taught.

BM—How can it be taught?

EM—A tougher question.

BM—Is it being taught?

EM—Not that I can discern.

BM—Then back to the previous question. How can it be taught?

EM—To educate undergraduates for citizenship requires a different orientation from that which is usual in academia. The basis for analysis of what needs to be offered to students should become not primarily academic or professional certification but also practice in the world. To prepare for this different orientation, I suggest we begin by holding some conversations about what is most important for a good education in the civic arts. I can envision a series of conversations between community activists, local elected officials, journalists who cover politics, and some political thinkers (some of whom are academics). The results of those conversations, prepared for general sharing by the listeners, could then be discussed with people selected for their wisdom about the public life, whether they be academics or not. That is, the conversation starts with those who know the area from their experience, and then engages with those who have thought about such experiences. The next step would be to bring the results of both sets of conversations to those who could teach or have taught courses on civic education on campuses, along with those whose support for such courses is essential (e.g., academic officers). The focus of this third set of conversations would be formulation of material directly helpful to teachers. Throughout, it is critical to find out not just what people say, but what they mean, to pull out the theory that is implicit in their practices and beliefs, to explore the practice that is implied by their theory and their ways of constructing knowledge. It is also essential to practice and prepare for good pedagogy in any programs that may finally develop. People always learn better when they are, or are becoming, aware of the predispositions they bring with them into the learning situation. And in looking for the mutual implications of theory and practice in the thinking of activists and academics, we are ourselves practicing good pedagogy—pedagogy appropriate to the political realm in which equals engage with each other in discussion and action that always have both theoretical and practical meaning, implications, consequences.

BM—My own impression is that the social scientists have done a better job than the philosophers in the kind of integrated, issue-oriented thinking you recommend. Do you agree?

EM—Yes and no. I am a hard liner and a defender of the classics in the sense that I think they offer the indispensible paradigms of good thinking. Any theory that originates within the kinds of conversations presently going on in the academy, without the critique and perspective the philosophical tradition affords, may seem more connected, more responsive to our problems, but may in fact be part of the problem rather than part of the solution. I call for radical thinking, which means, among other things, that our thinking has to be tested against the best that has been thought. A lot of social theory is very shallow because it fails to do that.

BM—Part of what you seem to be saying is that in order to think, we have to rethink the intellectual heritage as a point of departure.

EM—That is what Dewey and Arendt did. I think all good thinking needs that dimension. In that sense, we are always starting all over.

BM—But hasn't that kind of thinker always been the lonely minority?

EM—The crucial question now is how to increase their numbers on the assumption that, given the kind of world we live in, if we don't have more of them, we won't be able to solve our problems.

BM—Ideally all citizens?

EM—Ideally, yes.

BM—Do you count large numbers of such people among your friends and acquaintances?

EM—They do exist. Part of what keeps me interested in the problems of education and devoted to the peculiar kind of graduate school I work for is precisely that they do exist. One of our problems is that we tend to look for the best thinking in academia. That is not always the case. Some would argue that it is rarely the case, that academia is not conducive to radical thought.

BM—It does seem to be the case that academics aren't interested in ideas. That was the thesis of a recent book by Russell Jacoby called The Last Intellectuals. *He argues that the kind of thinker who is well grounded in culture and able to work back and forth between theory and the nitty-gritty issues of the day is a disappearing species.*

EM—Look at how academics get to be academics. They go through a graduate program that is highly specialized; they thus become firmly established in a discipline and, as professionals, work within it; they teach their specialty within a department framework; and they publish within the accepted canons of the profession. And what they publish is indicative of the impoverishment of their thought. I can't read those journals. I dislike them intensely. The articles in them are stylistically interchangeable. There is no person present thinking. They display certain analytic skills, sometimes with a little dry wit in imitation of the British. This stripping away of the contextual that leaves nothing but the skeleton of word play and analysis is an incredibly bad model of rationality. The kind of thinking that is necessary for citizenship in the kind of world we live in is marginalized if not throttled altogether by it. No wonder Socratic types tend to operate outside of the system.

BM—*Given the freedom, how would you design an ideal course?*

EM—When I have the luxury of teaching whatever I want, as I sometimes do, I teach my little shelf of favorite books.

BM—*What is on your little shelf?*

EM—Some Arendt, to be sure. I like her essays best for teaching purposes, and one in particular, called "Thinking and Moral Considerations," is a jewel. She dedicated that lecture to W. H. Auden, who was her very good friend. Also some Dewey. I particularly like his *Art as Experience* which summarizes the main tenets of his philosophy. And William James in a collection of his essays called *Pragmatism*. I emphasize his notion of radical empiricism. Glenn Gray's *The Warriors* is a beautiful example of someone attempting to understand the extraordinarily complex phenomenon of modern war. I also use a pair of novels, Philip Hallie's *Lest Innocent Blood Be Shed* and Albert Camus's *The Plague*. Other novels that work well are Alice Walker's *Meridian* (that novel alone, which is an effort to think through the civil rights issue in an unblinking fashion, puts her in the front ranks of political thinkers) and anything by Toni Morrison.

BM—*Some Sartre, maybe, as an example of the politically engaged thinker?*

EM—For some reason, Sartre doesn't appeal to me. I like Camus much better. And I use Simone de Beauvoir. Her novels don't blow me away, but there are parts of *The Second Sex* that are very good. She does a lot of thinking through in that book and comes up with categories which she both discovered and enriched. One of them is the category of the "other" to denote man's way of referring to women. I find that very illuminating. And lately, I have been using Simone Weil, the French mystic and political writer.

BM—*She surely is off the beaten path.*

EM—She is, but I like her very much, especially her idea of attentiveness to the phenomenon, by which she meant a respect for and a deep understanding of things as they are. Her mysticism was of a sort that tries to penetrate phenomena to a pure order behind them. But at the same time, she could write brilliant political articles. I find this conjunction of the political and the mystical powerful.

BM—*Wasn't it Charles Peguy who said everything begins in poli-*

tics and ends in mysticism?

EM—I don't know that. But I like it.

BM—Do any American thinkers combine mysticism and the concrete that way?

EM—James did. And I think Arendt did too. Elizabeth Young-Bruehl's biography of her is entitled *For Love of the World.* That catches it, the two poles of love or the mystical and the world or the phenomenal.

BM—This is a pretty exciting notion. Say a little more about mysticism. Does it have a religious connotation?

EM—No. Religion drives back to ideology. Mysticism helps you get out of the way of what it is you are trying to understand and enables you to concentrate on the specific. It is mind clearing. For Weil, I think it was simply the sum total of those mental exercises that enabled her to see things deeply and surely.

BM—A kind of this-worldly mysticism.

EM—Yes. And I find it has educational implications. When we try to teach students, we are trying to get them to think. And in order to think, they have to clear their minds in order to concentrate on whatever it is they want to think about. So many of our educational practices clutter up the mind rather than clear it. The curriculum all too often is designed to give solutions before students understand the problem. I admire those thinkers, like those on my shelf, who start with a problem, move on to appropriate established systems of thought, then come back to wonder before the phenomenon and let it speak. Usually we do it backwards.

BM—I'm going to have to read some Simone Weil.

EM—I hope you enjoy her.   □

An Interview with
FRANK NEWMAN on

Restructuring Education

FRANK NEWMAN has had a distinguished career in higher education, as a teacher, a college president, an author, and an education policy expert. He earned two bachelor's degrees from Brown University, one in engineering and one in naval science, a master's degree in business from Columbia University, and a doctorate in history from Stanford. A truly liberal education, one might say! From 1967 to 1974, he served as director of university relations at Stanford and then became president of the University of Rhode Island, in which capacity he served until 1983. In the early seventies, he chaired two task forces for two Secretaries of Health, Education, and Welfare and in 1974, published the *Newman Report on Higher Education*. In 1983, he became a Presidential Fellow at the Carnegie Institute for the Advancement of Teaching and in 1985, authored *Higher Education and the American Resurgence*. At the heart of this report is a strong challenge to higher education to take up once again its historic mission of civic education and service to society. Dr. Newman is co-founder of Campus Compact, an organization designed to emphasize these goals. Since 1985, he has been president of the Education Commission of the States, a 21-year-old consortium of the states created to assist education and political leaders with policy analysis and implementation at all levels of education. In this position, Dr. Newman travels widely in this country and abroad. He likes to joke that his current address at any given time is United Airlines.

I discovered that there is more than a grain of truth in this. We began this interview on a resplendent fall day in Vermont, and I tracked Dr. Newman in a series of phone calls to Washington, Pennsylvania, Missouri, and back to Washington before meeting with him again when he came to Ohio Wesleyan to deliver a commencement address and receive an honorary degree. In his address, he reminded the graduating students of their obligation as members of a free people to work together for the common good, and he proposed to them one final test, a take home test, so to speak, that would be due in 1993. "If you fail," he joked, "I empower the president to withdraw your degree." Then he posed these questions to the class of 1988:

Have you, as you have gone through your first five years, devised a major new way of doing some aspect of your job that substantially improves what your organization is trying to accomplish? Have you gotten mad about one of those things that someone ought to do something about and organized yourself and others to do it? Have you participated in a political campaign rather than standing on the sidelines complaining about the candidates? Have you helped someone in trouble, someone who needs a person to care, to assist, and not to turn their back? Have you enjoyed what you are doing? Have you learned to smile yet? Smiling has a great advantage that it makes those around you nervous. Have you gotten involved in some regular volunteer effort, an effort that tests your capacity and gives you the chance to take risks and do good? Have you given some of your hard-earned money to Ohio Wesleyan? Have you voted in every election? In the last presidential election, only 52.6% of the eligible voters voted, and among the 18-24 year olds only 17% voted. And finally, have you agreed with yourself to do all these things and take credit for none of the above? Well, if you passed this, if you together mutually passed this test, we as a country will pass our test. So much depends on the intellectual skill, the political skill, the moral skill of our leaders. In this we depend so much on our universities. Some countries in times of trial turn to the military which you know. Others turn to the large businesses. In the United States our tradition is that we turn to education.

The citation that accompanied his honorary degree on that occasion is an eloquent summary of Frank Newman's contributions to higher education. It reads as follows:

In 1871 the great American poet Walt Whitman published a book entitled *Democratic Vistas* in which he said that what makes a society cohere is the power of great ideas. Ohio Wesleyan University honors Frank Newman today because his life illustrates the truth of what Whitman said. Frank Newman has understood that our educational institutions are where great ideas are principally generated and transmitted. He has understood that the strength of our educational institutions is the strength of our nation. He has understood that what we sow in the successor generation is what we reap in the adult population. He has understood that there is no more creative labor than building for the future. Above all, he has understood that the debate about education is a debate about the root values of American society. He has been at the center of that debate for many years. And where he has not found a debate he has started one. His contributions have been marked by passion, irony, humor, and, more than anything else, insight. Dr. Newman, in appreciation of your many contributions to education in America, we are well pleased to honor you today.

BM—What differences do you see in American education between the time you published your first report in 1974 and your recent Higher Education and the American Resurgence?

FN—There have been enormous changes, some of them encouraging and some of them not so encouraging. Some of the things I said in 1974 sound archaic today.

BM—Like what?

FN—For example, what I said then about barriers to education for women. Education is more inclusive today, in ways we didn't anticipate then; it has reached out not only to women but to older students, to minority students, and to larger numbers of students.

BM—What is the downside?

FN—We have drifted too far toward career education to the detriment of the liberal arts, although I think that is beginning to change. Also, after a strong start in the education of minorities, we have begun to slack off, particularly for blacks and Hispanics. Finally, we are if anything getting worse in the matter of civic education.

BM—What do you mean by "resurgence" in the title of your recent book?

FN—It refers to redefining ourselves as a world leader. After World War II we were the undisputed leader in everything. Now we are not. So the question is: How do we regain our position of leadership? This question is really what drives our concern with the reform of education and has precipitated the period of self-examination we are now going through.

BM—Such periods of reexamination are not infrequent in America.

FN—True, we have had similar periods before. For example, in the 1890s when we wrestled with the question of how to get industry under control. We worried about antitrust laws, child labor, and working conditions. Or the period from 1954 onward when the Brown decision set off a nationwide concern with race relations which culminated in the civil rights legislation in the sixties. We are now concerned with U.S. competition in an international world. But the question is not merely one of competition. It is a larger question of cooperation, of what role we can play in forming a global community. What is at stake is who Americans think they are and what values they represent. It is a complicated issue, and that is why it is such an intense issue, and, of course, it has profound implications for education. The Education Commission of the States works closely with governors who have been studying this whole issue very carefully, and they have concluded a couple of things. One is that the pattern of industry must change. There must be a different kind of management, a different kind of education for workers, and more involvement of workers in the decision-making process, and this will mean changes in how state governments are run. Secondly, what they most clearly agree upon is that we must improve the quality of education. This is now a movement that has become so powerful that it is sweeping all the forces of our life in front of it. Every single state has had at least one commission and sometimes more dealing with how to improve the quality of education.

BM—The quality of education is one of those expressions that can quite easily become a shibboleth. Could you be more concrete about what you mean by it?

FN—Let me begin with what I think are some false or inadequate approaches to the question of quality. When the debate began, the focus was on the test scores of students. Then we began to test teachers, and that practice has become widespread. The results have been pretty disastrous. About 20 percent of teachers fail even the simplest tests. And that raises questions about the quality of their degree and the nature of teacher education. But I want to point out we can't get off the hook by blaming departments of education. If a math teacher is incompetent it is not the fault of the department of education but the department of mathematics. So our whole educational system is implicated. I agree that testing for minimal competence is necessary, but we've got to do much more than that. Assessment alone will not get us very far. A second false approach is the moralistic one that has characterized much of the Reagan administration. We cannot solve the problem of quality by merely chastising educators and exhorting them to do better. I must admit, though, that Secretary of Education William Bennett is less moralistic than he used to be. For example, he is now disposed to more federal spending. The third bad approach is elitism. Much of what passes for education reform is undisguised elitism. There is a lot of that in Allan Bloom's book *The Closing of the American Mind*. He equates standards with elitism. I agree with him about standards, but I don't equate them with elitism.

BM—Has Bloom contributed anything to the debate?

FN—I think he got hold of a part of the debate we had lost sight of, which is to say, the problem of a common culture. We still haven't settled that.

BM—We are still on the question of quality. How do you define that in a positive sense?

FN—The Education Commission of the States is working with about 200 secondary schools, and we are trying to do three things. We want to make principals educational leaders; we want to involve teachers in their work in a more meaningful way; and we want students, as a result, to become more committed. There is a lot of isolation and alienation out there. Teachers rarely have anything to do with their principals and then only on routine administrative matters. They don't have much interaction with their colleagues either. So it isn't too surprising that they aren't involved with their students. There has to be more leadership, more recognition for work done, and more involvement on the part of all concerned.

BM—Can you report some success stories?

FN—I like to cite the example of a high school in Long Island City which is run by LaGuardia Community College. It is a school exclusively for dropouts, and in New York City over half the students drop out. Enrollment is limited to 500 students. They have to apply, and they have to work once they are admitted. Over 85 percent of the students graduate, which is a spectacular rate. When I visited the school recently, I asked the students what difference this school meant. They all said the same thing. They all said it was the first time anyone took them seriously or expected anything of them as students. When I visited the classrooms, there was a palpable climate of involvement. There was a lot of discussion; students were making presentations, working on independent projects, arguing with the teacher, breaking into small groups, and so forth. That is a good model of how schools can be restructured for quality.

BM—But is it a good model for mainline schools? It seems somewhat exceptional.

FN—It is a good model. Some of our best successes are in suburban schools which do the same thing.

BM—Is money a large factor in school reform? Suppose the starting salary of teachers was $30,000 a year. Wouldn't that attract a higher caliber of teacher?

FN—Money is a factor. The Education Commission of the States supports higher pay for teachers. But I wouldn't want to say that money is the most important factor.

BM—What is?

FN—As I indicated, there are two—leadership and teacher involvement.

BM—But aren't they in turn dependent upon adequate remuneration?

FN—Adequate, yes. But money is not the crucial factor. Money is not the most important thing in America. That case is not often made very convincingly, especially to students, but I believe it is true. There is a large reservoir of idealism that drives much of the good work that is done in this country.

BM—Do you have a list of changes you would like to see?

FN—Yes, but I'll tell you what it is only on condition that if you don't like it, you have to put forth your own.

BM—Agreed.

FN—OK. Here is what I think we must achieve at all levels of education. First, the knowledge base of our graduates is too limited. It is particularly limited in the area of the nature, the history and philosophy of the American political system. No democracy can dispense with this. Furthermore, we have today in our student body large numbers of immigrants who are unfamiliar with it. The largest two groups of immigrants to the United States are Hispanics and Asians, both of which come from nondemocratic traditions. So we have a large job of education here. I include the intellectual skills of writing, quantitative analysis, and reasoning. I would put science and technology high on the list. These more than anything else shape the kind of world we live in. Ask a general audience where the most robots are used today, and they will say Japan. Ask in what industry, and they will say the automobile industry. Right?

BM—Right.

FN—Wrong. There are more robots used in the United States than anywhere else, and they are used primarily in the banking industry. I put creativity and imagination high on my list. Why this? Because we are a different society than we were, and we are seeking not just for new technologies but for new ideas, new services, and new social structures. We need entrepreneurial skills of all kinds. We were once the center of mass production. But we no longer are. Lots of countries do that better than we do. We live in what Jim Hunt, the former governor of North Carolina, calls a cutting-edge economy—indeed, a cutting-edge society, where there is a great premium placed on creativity. This implies the ability to take risks and to change because risk and change are part of our everyday lives. My father worked for the telephone company all his life. Few people today stay at the same job all their lives. And finally, we must renew our capacity to educate for civic responsibility.

BM—That is a good list.

FN—But the odd thing about it, the thing that strikes you most forcibly about it, is that we are not meeting these objectives in our educational system. The knowledge base of our students is too narrow, their skills are inadequate, most of them are scientifically illiterate, we actually punish creativity, and civic education is a wasteland.

BM—What is your explanation for this?

FN—I have concluded that it has to do with the way we teach. The common perception is that education is a matter of transferring knowledge through lectures and curricular modules. Even if we limited our aims of education to knowledge transfer, and I am arguing for a great deal more than that, the lecture method is not the most efficient way of doing it. Yet the teaching profession is deeply wedded to the belief that it is. The thinking goes something like this: I have this knowledge, the student doesn't have it, my job is to pass it on, the best way to do this is to lecture. I made this point at a conference of academics just a few days ago. A professor took me to task and argued that there is an important distinction to be made between the life of the mind and the life of belief. What you are talking about, he told me—civic responsibility and creativity and the like, are all very nice, but they fall under the life of belief. It is the university's job to deal with the life of the mind. I expressed surprise that the distinction could be so neatly drawn. So I asked him how he communicated the life of the mind. Did he draw his students into discussion? Did he do field work? Oh, no, he said, I want a classroom where only *I* talk. I asked him why. He said because they (that is, the students) must understand the logic and nature and purpose of things. Well, I said, there is a problem with this. I explained that even if the professor was successful in doing this, he would still leave a lot out. The point I made was that we don't learn much by merely listening to a lecture about it. All the research shows that in a lecture students pay attention less than 25 percent of the time. When they participate, they pay attention about 75 percent of the time.

College education is nowhere near as exciting nor as effective as it could be. In many ways it is boring, particularly the classroom part. The student is expected to sit quietly in class, listen to a lecture, make notes with the purpose of memorizing not only the information about the subject being transmitted, but the interpretation that is provided in a predigested form.

BM—It seems to kill creativity as well.

FN—Yes. To become creative, one must practice being creative. To become a risk taker, one must try to take risks. Particularly in a world where constant change has become the norm, students must reject facile answers and predigested certainty. They must fashion their own conclusions, tentative as they may be, and their own plans for learning. Perhaps most crucial, if one is to understand the importance of judgment and the importance of responsibility, one must learn by attempting to make such judgments and acting responsibly.

There is no more critical task ahead for American higher education than to transform the undergraduate experience into a more active learning process.

BM—That's about as powerful an attack on the lecture system as I've heard.

FN—I mean it to be. A student cannot learn to reason solely by listening to a description of how a teacher or professor has reasoned. Lectures, at their best, transmit knowledge, but they are rarely inspiring. They seldom transform the experience of learning from the humdrum to a level of excitement that captures the student's attention.

BM—Are you saying that lectures are boring?

FN—They are most of the time. But worse, they breed cynicism. Students know that mastering data or a given professor's viewpoint is only peripherally related to the purposes of education, but intimately related to the grades necessary for admission to selective programs. That process can't help but breed cynicism.

BM—Can this problem be laid to the nature of graduate education?

FN—It can be laid to the educational system as a whole. When students go through a primary and secondary school system that is hierarchical and where their experience is largely passive, when they endure the same experience in college, and when they go on to graduate school, which is another period of intellectual subservience, what makes us think they are going to be different when they become teachers in their turn? The answer is nothing makes us think that and they don't. So clearly we must do something different. And we have to do it now.

BM—Do what?

FN—You can probably anticipate my answer. In my recent book, I argue hard for some form of national service to put teeth into our rhetorical bows to the ideal of civic education and to put some meat on the bones of the academic curriculum. In short, to give students a better education than they are getting now.

BM—Do you think students will go for this?

FN—My evidence shows that students want to participate more, but they have heard no signals from us. We have to send very different signals to the young people of our society. For all the cynicism about political life in this country, and for all the worry about the passiveness and self-interest of students, there is an abiding belief in America that some form of service is a proper step in the education of the young.

BM—Is that why you founded Campus Compact?

FN—Yes. The full title is Campus Compact: The Project for Public and Community Service. I co-founded it with the presidents of Stanford, Brown, and Georgetown Universities. It now has the active suport of over 100 university presidents who encourage their students to engage in such varied public service projects as teaching illiterates to read, reconstructing inner-city parks, providing health examinations for residents of low-income communities, and serving disadvantaged youth as Big Brothers and Big Sisters. I see signs that Campus Compact is going to grow by leaps and bounds.

BM—Can the government help?

FN—It sure can. We already have a model in the GI Bill and ROTC. What we need now is a GI Bill to provide students with aid in return for community services. Another approach would be to make community service a requirement for graduation at both the college and high school levels. Such measures could provide learning by doing in the best sense of the word.

BM—How do you argue the case for service to the more traditional academic?

FN—There are two arguments. One is that this has always been part of what we believe a liberal arts education ought to be. And going all the way back to the thirties there has been a variety of federal programs that responded to this belief, the best known of which was the Peace Corps. My strongest argument is that service learning responds to a capacity students have and one which we must respect. Not to respect it is to devalue the student. They are at an age when they have much to contribute to the work of society (and our present system has virtually made it impossible for them to make that contribution), and this in turn will contribute exponentially to their education in citizenship. This may be the common experience we are looking for.

BM—You clearly think this is an idea whose time is ripe.

FN—I do, most certainly.

BM—Some think it is too difficult to reform the present structure of higher education, that what you advocate through Campus Compact might be better accomplished through other organizations like

*the corporation or the military. Others argue that we need new
institutions of postsecondary education. What do you say to them?*

FN—To answer the first question first, there are a lot of freestand-
ing institutions that educate their membership in various ways. Adult
education is booming in this country. Labor unions do a lot of it, too.
As for developing alternate postsecondary institutions, we have done
some of that (for instance, the community colleges), but it doesn't
seem to be the way to go. The traditional educational structure is a
powerful magnetic force which like a magnet draws all within its
orbit. The thing to notice is that people who begin their education
elsewhere end up in a traditional college or university taking a
traditional degree.

*BM—Could we therefore conclude that this staying power is built
upon real merit?*

FN—People want two things from education: quality and prestige. And the traditional institutions are best able to deliver both. The
public has tremendous trust in educational institutions. You only
have to look at any graduation ceremony to see that.

*BM—You have been saying that education is in serious need of
reform, but now you seem to be saying that it has great vitality.*

FN—That isn't a contradiction. The reforms are necessary, but
within the framework of a traditional structure that does indeed
possess great vitality and capability for change, especially when
compared to universities in other countries.

BM—To what do you attribute this vitality.

FN—I could point to a lot of things. Let me make two points. For
one thing, universities guarantee intellectual freedom. That is a big
plus, and, while it is not uniquely an American invention, we don't
find it to the same degree in other countries, and, of course, in many
countries we don't find it at all. The universities are the home of
intellectual freedom and that is very important for our society.
Secondly, education is the most democratic of all the guarantees we
pledge to our citizens. The United States is not as advanced as some
other countries in guaranteeing things like housing, jobs, health care,
and the like. But we do deliver pretty well on giving everyone some
level of education and keeping that door open. We worry about
standards, but we also worry about accessibility, and we always have
to strike a balance between the two.

*BM—Are you worried about elitism in American higher educa-
tion? You disagreed with Bloom earlier on that, but isn't it a fact that*

*the best universities in the country are elitist, accepting only a small
percentage of their applicants?*

FN—There is a great variety of educational institutions in America, and the so-called elite universities don't educate most of the students. Moreover, the pool of applicants to these universities keeps changing. So the point is not that few get in, but that those who get in are constantly changing. I think even the most selective schools are open enough in this respect to avoid the charge of elitism.

*BM—We'll put that one on the back burner for further argument
at another time. But before time runs out, we want to probe a couple
of other areas. You are very sanguine about change in American
education, about both the possibility and the quality of change. How
do you answer the oft-repeated charge that the changes are merely
cosmetic and that there hasn't been a significant change in the last 50
years, a kind of* plus ça change, plus c'est la même chose *syndrome?*

FN—Not guilty. Change is constant, it is qualitative, and it is cumulative. And change almost always takes place according to the same pattern. It is rarely internally driven. The impetus for change comes from the public. Academics react to the call for change somewhat as follows: At first they say it can't be done, that it's a violation of academic freedom or whatever; secondly, they say it isn't practical; then they say it will cost too much; and when the change is finally accomplished, they say it was their idea all along. I have a wonderful story to illustrate my point. When the GI Bill was introduced in 1943, there was a series of hearings. I've gone back and read the legislative history on this. It's very interesting. Every university president who testified was against it. Hutchins of Chicago was against it. Conant of Harvard was against it. They said it would lower the quality of education, it would let the barbarians within the ivory gates, and so forth. The academics were wrong in every single respect. But today you can't find an academic who does not believe that the GI Bill was the greatest thing ever and that the academic community brought it into being. And speaking of the GI Bill, it alone suffices to answer the charge that no substantial changes take place in American education.

*BM—That's an interesting point you make about the impetus for
educational change coming from outside. Say a little more about
that.*

FN—A view common among academics is that the academy functions apart from society but provides society with a much-needed service. The belief is deeply rooted that they decide how the young shall be educated. But this is not true and has never been true in the United States. The power over the content and purposes of education is vested in the public, delegated by the public to lay trustees who, in turn, delegate it to the president who, finally, delegates it to the faculty. And what the public has traditionally demanded is implementation of policy to meet broad public purposes. That was clearly stated at the founding of the first university in America in 1636. The Morrill Act is also a good illustration. At the time, it was clearly in society's interest to emphasize the agricultural and mechanical arts. When Cornell was founded, there was a great debate about what students there should study. The legislature was very firm in calling for the teaching of morality. Today there is a call for quality and creativity and service. Educators are the implementers, holding in trust for the public the curriculum.

BM—Isn't the public somewhat fickle, now demanding this, now that, and in all events demanding a winning football team?

FN—All along the way there has been tension between the liberal and the pragmatic. The pendulum swings. But we have never wavered in our public perception that the liberal arts are central. We believe in pragmatic goals, but the liberal arts are one of the ways we get there.

BM—Doesn't that reverse the historical view which considers the liberal arts of intrinsic rather than instrumental value?

FN—When we examine the historical record carefully, it is clear that education has always served social purposes. When you think about it, you realize it could not be otherwise. □

An Interview with
ROBERT PAYTON on
Education, Social Discourse, and Philanthropy

WHEN I first interviewed Robert Payton late in 1985, he was president of the Exxon Education Foundation, a position he assumed on March 1, 1977. Since then, he has become director of the Center on Philanthropy and professor of philanthropic studies at Indiana University. Payton has also served as president of Hofstra University and C.W. Post College and was U.S. ambassador to the Federal Republic of Cameroon from 1967 to 1969. He was educated at the University of Chicago and was on the faculty of Washington University in St. Louis for nine years, part of that time (1961-66) as vice chancellor.

Robert Payton has a unique perspective on American education, seeing, as he does, philanthropy not only as the glue that binds all our educational efforts together, but also as the key to understanding the meaning of America. "Without an understanding of the philanthropic tradition, it is not possible to understand American society," he states flatly. It is a large claim, and one he justifies with great energy and persuasive arguments in this interview. This theme taps into the vision of America described by Alexis de Tocqueville in the 1830s (de Tocqueville attributed the energy of the young republic to the

American genius for forming voluntary associations) and, more broadly, into the tradition of civic humanism that was one of the informing currents of the American founding. The general thesis of civic humanism, which has deep historical roots but was elaborated by thinkers of the Italian Renaissance, holds that we become fully human only by participating in civic life. More and more, I have come to think that we cannot make the case of liberal education without at the same time making the case for citizenship. I might even go so far as to argue that by making the case for citizenship in a democratic society, we make the strongest case for liberal education. The difficulty has always been to tie the two together in a convincing manner. Payton does that as well as anyone I know.

BM—How does the education scene look from the forty-sixth floor of the Exxon building?

RP—I think this is a very interesting period in education. It began some years ago as a reaction to all the rapid changes and challenges to our received values. For a while there in the mid-seventies, we were spinning our wheels, but then we began a process of reconsideration that made the present situation very promising.

BM—What have we reconsidered?

RP—Some of the best thinking going on at the present time is about general education. We are trying to rearticulate what that might be. I think this is a healthy exercise any time, but particularly at this time when careerism in the baccalaureate program is pronounced, respect for the humanities at an all-time low, and the specter of retrenchment haunts many institutions.

BM—What progress have we made?

RP—When I became president of Hofstra University in 1973, I said in my inaugural speech that the principal task facing American higher education was to make general education central to the curriculum. I came here in 1977 and made an effort to commit the Exxon Education Foundation to this task. It was my judgment, based on what I observed around the country, that this was an appropriate area for us to be involved in. Between 1977 and 1983, something like two-thirds of all institutions of higher education have been engaged in some formal reconsideration of general education. This process, of course, began earlier in some institutions, but it really matured around 1980. I believe the heart of liberal education is general education, and to be confused about the one is to be confused about the other. We are now, I think, moving into the second stage of this process, moving beyond concern into implementation. One interesting place I see this happening is in professional education. Many of the professions are worried about the narrowly specialized education their members receive. This is true of engineering, medicine, law, and business, and in advanced study in the arts and sciences. It is true in prestige institutions as well as in those of lesser renown. I think this may be at the forefront of our thinking about general education, although it will probably take us another decade to think it all the way through.

BM—Are you saying "think through" what we mean by general education or professional education or the relationship between the two?

RP—The relationship between the two. What I am saying is that we have to work from the dissatisfactions in the professional schools back down through the system to questions of general education at the undergraduate level and even in the high schools and elementary schools.

BM—So it is a top-down process?

RP—In a sense, yes. The graduate schools and the professional schools are going to have to say to undergraduate educators what it is that they think has gone wrong. We have to decide what to do at what level, at what stage the non-technical dimensions of professional education are best dealt with. For example, can you deal with ethical questions when ethics is introduced as either an elective or a minimal requirement only at the level of advanced professional education? Or does the ethical dimension have to appear in a much more conscious and coherent way much earlier in the educational process? But don't misunderstand me. I am not trying to press general education into some particular time frame. I think general education should go on all the time, at every level, and it should continue throughout one's lifetime. General education has to do not only with skills, but habits of mind, attitudes, and values of intellectual behavior, with questioning and exploring kinds of attitudes and habits of mind. General education provides the framework within which the social system is both understood and questioned. It is the place where the society and the educational system come together. I call general education education for social thought and discourse.

BM—Could you elaborate on that concept?

RP—Well, it gets back to the problem of specialization. In recent years, overspecialization in the humanities and social sciences has become a serious intellectual problem. The case I want to argue is that these disciplines should, if they are properly conceived and taught, determine the quality of how we think about and talk about our society as a whole. The humanities and the social sciences are the repository of the most important ideas of human society. It is here that one learns about good and evil, justice and injustice, about how to read and write, speak and listen, how to express and persuade, prove and demonstrate. There is an underlying ethic of great social importance behind double-entry bookkeeping. Or, to take another example, behind the debates over budget allocations are profound and serious issues of the conflicting aspirations of access and excellence in higher education. To understand and to reformulate the issues (the problem of social thought) and to reconcile differing opinions about them (the problem of discourse) require knowledge of history and philosophy as well as of economics and politics. The difficulty of tracing the paths that ideas follow as they work their way into our minds and values and attitudes and express themselves in our votes and our purchases makes the ideas no less important. In fact, the very difficulty of tracing these ideas, of predicting their consequences, probably makes them even more powerful. We are particularly vulnerable to our ignorance.

BM—If the faculty is overspecialized and overspecialization leads to ignorance, then the inescapable logic of your position would seem to be that the faculty are ignorant.

RP—Miseducated rather than ignorant. The systematic miseducation of the faculty is a problem that will occupy us for the next generation.

BM—There is presumably some connection between the miseducation of the faculty and the deterioration of social discourse.

RP—Oh, yes! Higher education almost seems at times to be dominated by technocrats and Marxists. Neither has developed, nor can they develop, an adequate language of social discourse. Technocrats are limited by the artificial cognitive boundaries they place around the disciplines. They have created a structure that makes it very difficult for students to relate what they are learning to the world about them. They have to relate instead to the structure that the faculty has created. That is why education tends to get reduced to mechanics: the mechanics of testing, of curriculum building, of administration, etc. The Marxists, for their part, are limited by ideological blinders. I might note in passing that Marxist studies are a cottage industry on campuses today.

BM—Do you take that to be a bad omen?

RP—Perhaps not in and of itself. But I am bothered by the fact that America's most distinctive tradition does not have comparable prominence and visibility.

BM—What tradition do you refer to?

RP—The philanthropic tradition—voluntary service, voluntary association, voluntary giving. It does indeed make a difference to our thinking about society whether one sees legitimacy only in the state or in the marketplace. Philanthropy as it is organized in the United States provides a potent means for social change. It is a subject that touches the life of every student and every faculty member on every American campus. It is easily related to every discipline of the humanities and social sciences, and indeed to the hard sciences as well, and to professional studies like medicine, law, and business. It permeates American life. It provides the resources for some of the most important activities that give shape and substance to our efforts to be a free and open and democratic society. Yet, inexplicably, it is not a matter of central intellectual concern. It could be taught, it should be taught, but it is not taught.

BM—There aren't many people who link together the ideas of education, social values, and philanthropy the way you do. Are you a minority of one?

RP—A minority, yes, but our numbers are growing. I recently wrote a major position paper on this subject for the independent sector and have harped on it in various articles and speeches. I make two basic points about philanthropy. On the one hand, it is part of the religious tradition of good works and charitable giving with roots in the Bible. My second point is that philanthropy is essential to the preservation of an open and free society. From this point of view, it is a central democratic virtue because it directs our attention to the needs of others and makes us individually and collectively responsible for the relief of human suffering as well as improvement of the human condition.

BM—Wasn't it Andrew Carnegie who said that the purpose of making money is to give it away?

RP—I think so. But John D. Rockefeller put the point even better. The best philanthrophy, he said, "is the investment of effort, time, and money to expand and develop the resources at hand, and to give opportunity for progress and healthful labor where it did not exist before. No more money giving is comparable to this in its lasting and beneficial results." This is close to the point made by Maimonides in the twelfth century.

BM—I hear you saying that we cannot understand American society without understanding the philanthropic tradition.

RP—Right. And that is the primary reason why the study of philanthropy should have a place in education, particularly at the undergraduate level. But it is not the only reason. A second important reason can be cast in the terms of self-interest usually employed to attract students to professional programs. More people are employed in the nonprofit, voluntary, independent, philanthropic sector than by the federal and state governments combined. This means that one out of twelve students on the average will be employed in some area of the philanthropic sector.

BM—Didn't de Tocqueville touch on this when he wrote about voluntary association?

RP—Yes, voluntary associations are very much part of what we mean by philanthropy.

BM—Is philanthropy important in non-Western cultures as well, or even in other Western countries?

RP—Voluntary action for public purposes now appears in new formative stages in socialist countries, in faltering welfare states, and in even the poorest among the developing countries of the Thrid World. New nongovernmental associations appear in the climate of *glasnost* in the Soviet Union; British universities organize fund-raising from alumni and forge new alliances with business corporations for support of research; new nontribal voluntary associations deal with problems that neither the government nor the marketplace attend to in Africa. Within the United States, there is new recognition among blacks and Hispanics of the importance of their own philanthropic traditions to their own social and economic development.

BM—There is obviously a direct connection between a democratic capitalist economy and the philanthropic tradition. Maybe academics don't appreciate the latter because they are generally critical of the former.

RP—I think that is true, at least for some.

BM—This might be seen as particularly vicious form of biting the hand that feeds you. Most educational institutions couldn't exist without philanthropy.

RP—Yes. When Rockefeller wrote the words I cited a moment ago, he had already contributed some 35 million dollars to establish the University of Chicago.

BM—*How do you explain the academic bias against capitalism?*

RP—Academics who are charged with a bias against capitalism are often merely acting quite legitimately as critics. Some, however, are critical of capitalism while blind to its advantages and naively uncritical of the available alternatives. Bias of this sort isn't limited to academics and other intellectuals; it is just more objectionable among those who should know better. I find more interesting— because less fully discussed—the widespread academic discomfort with philanthropy. That's a subject worth, of an E.D. Hirsch.

BM—*Not only discomfort, but downright ignorance.*

RP—I can agree with that. We know less about our philanthropic tradition than we know even about geography, for example, and we know little enough about that. We are increasingly philanthropically illiterate.

BM—*Whence the need to study it. How would you organize a course in philanthophy?*

RP—First of all, I would take as a title a phrase from the anthropologist Clifford Goertz, and call it "The Social History of the Moral Imagination." The course would trace the roots of the tradition back to the Old Testament mandate to care for the widowed, the orphaned, the homeless, and the poor. I would turn to Greece and Rome for the origin of ideas on endowments and foundations and the tradition of honor linked to service to the community. I would then ask students to explore the ways in which the modern world has expanded and developed the philanthropic agenda. How has reform come about? Who was it who first saw what others had only looked at, and began to work for the abolition of slavery, for prison reform, for an end to child labor, for civil rights, for the environment? How did these ideas find their way into the public consciousness and onto the legislative docket? Where did the idea of the social responsibility of business corporations come from? How has that idea developed over the century given to the humanizing of the American business corporation? And all along the way, we would ask ourselves why it is that this tradition has fared so well in American society and has yielded so easily to a marginal role elsewhere.

BM—*Can you give us some idea of what is actually being taught on this subject?*

R P—The academic center of philanthropic studies that I know best, the new Center on Philanthropy at Indiana University, has set a "comprehensive" agenda for itself. It has three programmatic divisions: an academic division, a research division, and a public service division. The agendas of research and public service are relatively straightforward. Research in philanthropy has been under way at the Program on Non-Profit Organizations at Yale University for more than ten years. More than a decade before that, historian Merle Curti established a program of research in philanthropy at the University of Wisconsin. The Research Committee of Independent Sector publishes a biennial report that identifies almost a thousand projects. The public service division at Indiana embraces education and training in fund-raising, nonprofit organization and management, and other practical matters for which the demand appears to be insatiable. Case Western Reserve University's Mandel Center on Non-Profit Organizations is best known among the several new centers in this sector of the field. There are new programs to serve midcareer professionals and new programs to serve the countless, often small, and fragile organizations for which they work. Public policy research is an important aspect of the new Center on Philanthropy and Voluntarism at Duke University. The practical and professional dimensions of philanthropic studies are driven by demand in the marketplace.

BM—What about at the undergraduate level?

R P—Philanthropy in undergraduate education is another matter. Discovery of the field as a field is very recent. Two years ago, the American Association of Fund Raising Councils provided start-up funds for a project of the Association of American Colleges (AAC). A competition generated several dozen new courses. Those proposed (including those funded) were grounded in a wide variety of disciplines and institutions. Reading those proposals provides the most convenient short course in what American faculty members with some interest in philanthropy think about how the subject should be taught.

BM—So there is growth in the field?

R P—Yes. If ten years ago there were fewer than five courses in the nation dealing with philanthropy as a subject of the general education of undergraduates, today there may be as many as fifty. A recent AAC report on general education counts thirty-eight thousand courses in women's studies, by comparison. The place of women's studies, even so, remains a matter of debate, and that suggests that the place of philanthropic studies in the curriculum will remain an open issue for some years, perhaps decades.

BM—What are the principal obstacles you encounter in trying to develop courses on philanthropy?

RP—Well, there are quite a few. I divide them into practical problems and theoretical problems.

BM—Let's take the practical problems first.

RP—They are pretty obvious: the lack of qualified teachers, the shortage of classroom tested materials, lack of institutional support, poor visibility for the subject, and the like.

BM—And the theoretical problems?

RP—There are three main ones. The first grows out of the interdisciplinary character of the subject; the second raises the difficult problem of advocacy, ideology, and bias; and the third derives from the inescapable links between philanthropic theory and history, on the one hand, and philanthropic practice and organization, on the other.

BM—Say something about each of these problems.

RP—The study of philanthropy should be interdisciplinary. It draws on all the humanities and social sciences and on many of the professions. Education in philanthropy arises out of the exploration of open-ended social issues—those persistent and recurrent questions that dominate public consciousness and discourse. Such issues are often confused rather than clarified by the narrow focus of specialization. The current environmental agenda mentioned earlier, for example, or the social agendas of homelessness, AIDS, drug abuse, domestic violence, and illiteracy do not lend themselves to treatment in the tidy categories of departments and schools, disciplines and professions. Open-ended social issues tend to show up instead in messy, sometimes marginal centers and institutes, which is, I suspect, where they belong. Philanthropy qualifies as one of Clifford Goertz's "blurred genres," drawing on the insights and methods of anthropology and literature and religion and economics.

BM—Would you agree that courses on philanthropy could be taught within existing departments?

RP—Yes, they could be, although I don't think that is ideal. But I would be quite comfortable with departmental courses dealing, for example, with the question of desert in courses in moral philosophy;

dealing with poverty and the poor laws in courses in social history; dealing with the role of interest groups in courses offered by political scientists who view voluntary action for public purposes as essential to the American political tradition; dealing with the clash of egoism and altruism. As with those who advance women's studies and environmental studies and other such fields, my colleagues and I hope to win recognition for the study of philanthropy as a serious field of intellectual inquiry in its own right and to see it turn up appropriately in the rest of the curriculum as well.

BM—What about the advocacy issue?

RP—That is more controversial. Some colleagues have expressed justifiable concern that the study of philanthropy is being pressed as a device to raise money or as a form of self-congratulation. The fact is that the shallow endorsement of the philanthropic tradition can lead to serious confusion. The serious study of the history of philanthropy reveals how difficult it is to accomplish high-minded goals and how often well-intended charitable initiatives have resulted in harm to the recipients. Philanthropic studies should be at least as well prepared to engage in self-examination and self-criticism as are women's studies, for example, or Marxist studies, or free enterprise studies, or even religious studies. An important but different matter of bias— better talked about than whispered—is the allegation of institutional pressure on faculty members to avoid offending past, present, and prospective donors. Some academics seem to feel that the only way they can prove their virtue is to attack all benefactors in the style of Thorstein Veblen (alas, often with the sarcasm but without the style). Dwight MacDonald's description of the Ford Foundation as a "vast body of money surrounded by people who want it" is a reminder that strength of character is required on both sides of a philanthropic relationship. Thirty years in, out, and around the academic world has persuaded me that no field is immune to Faustian bargaining of one kind or another. Philanthropy will have to be as rigorous and conscientious in dealing with its blind spots and its habits of group-think as every other field—certainly no less, and perhaps no more.

BM—And, finally, a word about the problem of theory and practice.

RP—I'll confine myself to two brief remarks here. First, if we contend that voluntary service helps students to better understand social and economic class relations, for example, it seems reasonable to link observation of behavior—that is, observation of practice—

outside the classroom with ideas and theories advanced inside the classroom. (How do people treat one another in a philanthropic relationship? How well do students recognize and understand their own attitudes?) Few fields are better equipped for such inquiry than philanthropic studies; every campus has its own voluntary associations as well as close links to others in the community nearby. It is also useful to bring together scholars and practitioners in studying philanthropy. Every professional field struggles—for the most part unsuccessfully—with the often incompatible demands of these uneasy allies. Those in the humanities and social sciences remember recent awkward experiences with providing intellectual services to corporations or to government agencies or to the media. Yet some of the most interesting educational innovations of recent years have come from efforts to bring scholars and practitioners together— bringing the insights of moral philosophers to discussions of ethics in government and business or to decisions of medical practitioners in hospitals, to cite the most familiar examples.

BM—I take it you are relatively optimistic about the future of the field?

RP—Relatively, yes. We've made a good start at establishing beachheads in academia. We also have a new journal in the field called *Chronicle of Philanthropy*. Behind all of this is the weight of hundreds and even thousands of years of tradition, the awakening interest of imperiled organizations, the demonstrated power of voluntary action when it is effectively mobilized. None of that will suddenly disappear, any more than governments will suddenly discover the secret of omnipotent wisdom or the marketplace will suddenly reveal the secret of human happiness. What happens next will determine whether we pass the tradition along in better health than it was transmitted to us. That alone seems sufficient to justify the effort to bring philanthropy into the intellectual lives of undergraduates.

BM—It occurs to me that philanthropy might be seen as a middle term between general education and the professions, which are primarily responsible for generating the wealth that makes philanthropy possible.

RP—A good suggestion.

BM—To return to that subject, what promising signs do you see linking the problems of general education with the concerns of professional education? Can you point to some breakthroughs?

RP—We are very encouraged by the leadership shown by Derek Bok, the president of Harvard University. He has challenged three of the most influential professional schools there—medicine, law, and business—to take a look at what they are doing. The Exxon Education Foundation made a grant last year to the Harvard Medical School to pursue the problem of the general education of physicians, physicians understood as full and complete human beings, in the full range of their existence, and not merely as specialists. Harvard doesn't think it is good medicine if it is medicine learned and practiced in too specialized a way. Then you lose human understanding and the physician is less of a physician. Harvard has begun what they call their "new pathway" with 25 selected first-year medical students, all Oliver Wendall Holmes scholars. Their purpose is to provide a model of how professional education might be changed to make room for larger ends.

BM—Has anything been published on this project?

RP—The medical school has put out some general material for the Harvard community that is available to anyone who is interested. The question they are asking is: What is the best education for a physican, all things considered? This question grows out of a sense of some deficiencies in medical education that show up in the relationship of the physician to the patient and to others with whom he has to interact. They are asking, "What are we doing here that might be done differently?" without denigrating—and it is very important to recognize this—the scientific and technological requirements of modern medical education and research. They will intend to produce physicians who can do independent research and remain intellectually on top of their fields. So it's a very tough problem. A strong case will have to be made because there are enormous pressures on students already. It is easy to talk about such reform, but it will be very difficult to achieve. We feel that if some progress can be made in a place as competitive, selective, and intensive as the Harvard Medical School, then other professions, there and elsewhere, stand a better chance of benefiting from what they have learned. Physicians, like other professionals, are concerned with many values like self-esteem, ambition, prestige in the community, relations with peers, moral considerations, and much more that falls into the nebulous "non-technical" area. So the boundaries of the problem are by no means clear cut. But for me that's what general education ought to address.

BM—Are other professions as far along in this re-examination as the medical profession?

RP—That's hard to say. I alluded earlier to the corporate social responsibility debate. The corporation has gone a long way down the road of re-examining its social role in the context of values. From what I hear, the engineering profession is on its way. The dean of Virginia Tech asked some dozen alumni, all of whom were trained as engineers and all of whom were operating as chief executive officers of large corporations, what advice they would give entering freshmen. Almost all of them said two things. First, engineering students should continue to get a good education in their field, and, second, they should do everything they can to get as much education as possible in the areas of verbal skills and human relations. Very little in current engineering programs meet those latter requirements. The programs do very well what they set out to do; namely, to produce technically competent engineers who are highly marketable professionals after four years of undergraduate education. Engineering is probably the most demanding of all undergraduate programs (not the most competitive, but the most demanding). The downside of this is the high price the engineer pays in the nontechnical aspects of his education. Engineers who suceed in the higher echelons of corporate life, and many do, do so on their wits, their energy, and their ambition, and not because of their undergraduate educational background in engineering. They overcome their limitations. Those who don't, find themselves in mid-career at a plateau, and are unlikely to rise above it.

BM—What are some other issues that are occupying you these days?

RP—Our plate is full—too full, probably. I will cite only one broad problem that will probably be of greatest interest to your readers: Demographic and cultural changes and what those changes imply for democratic values—the continuing test of American exceptionalism. It is a subject that is both conceptually difficult and terribly sensitive to talk about. Yet it is at the center of what many of us believe to be the most important educational problem of the age: the idea of citizenship in a multicultural society.

BM—Do you think it is the case that most education reform is coming from outside the academy—from foundations, for example, or from the government or public opinion?

RP—Clark Kerr said 25 years ago that the great changes in the university have always come from the world outside it. I agree with that. What interests me most is how the nonprofit organizations act as the source of social change. People with ideas want to act in the public interest and come together in associations that need resources. When the ideas are found timely and persuasive and there is effective organization, such volunteers have enormous influence. Politicians and bureaucrats and merchants and manufacturers and academics are stimulated to respond, to catch up with the way these people have altered the public agenda. This is the genius of our system, and its conscience as well.

BM—We thank you.   □

An Interview with
DOUGLAS SLOAN on

Educating the Imagination

IN Genesis, God is encountered as a creator. That men and women are created in the divine image is another way of saying that creativity is the first born of our human gifts, a genuine mark of divinity in us. That has been a common perception among thinkers from Plato to modern times. Plato argued that the greatest benefits come to us through that creative madness which is the gift of the gods. Many prophets and poets, he pointed out, conferred splendid boons on Greece when under the divine spell but did little or nothing when they were in their "right" minds. In modern times, philosophers like Alfred North Whitehead have affirmed the primacy of creativity. Whitehead, in fact, asserted that creativity is the ultimate brute fact of existence, the most basic general character of nature. If, says Whitehead, all the characteristics of nature were abstracted, one by one, there would result a final residual element from which no further abstraction could be accomplished. This final element is creativity.

Few would deny that creativity ought to be one of the aims of education, perhaps *the* aim. Yet it rarely is. A good argument could be made to the contrary: that education diminishes creativity. There are creative people in our society, but not everyone would argue that the society itself is creative. Science is no doubt at the cutting edge of creativity in modern times, but it is so often at odds with genuine creativity. Douglas Sloan wrestles with that paradox in the following interview. On the one hand, science stands in the forefront of our intellectual efforts. On the other, it is the root cause of some of our major problems. Like Puritanism, to which science is so much indebted, it rests upon an ethic that is at once compelling and vicious. Caught betwixt and between, as it were, education struggles valiantly to ground such core concepts as cognition, civic responsibility, and personhood.

Douglas Sloan, a specialist in the history of religion and education in American culture, is Professor of History and Education at Teachers College of Columbia University, Adjunct Professor of Religion and Education at the Union Theological Seminary in New York City, and immediate past editor of *Teachers College Record*, a well regarded journal in the field of education. Dr. Sloan's books include *The Scottish Enlightenment and the American College Ideal*, *The Great Awakening and American Education*, and *Education and Values*. Most recently his *Insight-Imagination*, to which reference is made in the interview, was published by the Greenwood Press.

BM—What is there in your intellectual history that accounts for your interest in the problems of education?

DS—As an undergraduate, I was a chemistry and philosophy major. In the late fifties, I studied theology at Yale and in Germany. I then dropped theology altogether and went to Columbia to do a Ph.D. in history. From there, I went to Teachers College as a professor of history and education. I soon discovered that many of the old theological questions kept coming up in new guises.

BM—It seeems to be a fact that many of our problems wear a theological face. A while back, we interviewed Ted Fiske of The New York Times. *He did graduate work in political science and theology and told us that he found political science helpful when covering religion, and theology helpful in covering education. What were some of the theological problems that kept recurring?*

DS—The whole question of the goals and purposes of education, for example. This is a question of meaning which has firm theological roots and a question which no one can escape asking. It carries us beyond a concern with means and techniques that dominates so much contemporary philosophy of education. Questions of purpose aren't raised very often in modern education, but I find them the most interesting and most important questions.

BM— You begin your book with a discussion of science and seem to be arguing that science sets the intellectual pace of our culture, that science rather than theology raises the important value questions. You might want to say that science is itself in important ways an extension of the theological tradition. Some people hold that view. Lynn White for one says that the enterprise of science is cast in the matrix of Christian theology.

DS—The problem I am trying to address is the assumption that science is the only legitimate source of knowledge about the world. To the extent that this view is dominant, it defines the kind of world we come to know. Our choices about the ways of knowing are restricted by this one way of knowing; it determines the framework within which we ask all our questions.

BM—Isn't that a somewhat parochial view? It is no doubt true that the scientific paradigm has shaped the Western academic mind. But that isn't the whole world. Most the world's population hasn't been affected by science.

DS—But most of the world is being affected by it. The leaders in traditional cultures today are the new technocrats, many of whom were trained in the West. I do indeed think this is a parochial view. That is part of my argument. But not quite in the way you indicated. Traditional values everywhere are under assault. People are having enormous difficulties trying to adjust their values to a scientific worldview.

BM—And part of your argument is also that the values of scientific culture are not adequate substitutes for traditional values.

DS—Only in the narrowest sense. Scientific values tend to be utilitarian, materialistic, quantitative, and functionalist. They provide little place for the values and personal-social commitments necessary for a rich and life-enhancing existence. My point is not that science is value free—that claim is mistaken—but that its values are too shallow.

BM—On the other hand, you take pains to note the many benefits bestowed by science. Sometimes you talk as though scientific values are superior to those they replaced. Is this an ambiguity in our own mind?

DS—I have trouble with science only when exorbitant claims are made for it, as is happening in the modern world. But I recognize that science is an important development in the evolution of human consciousness. The ambiguity isn't in my understanding of the situation but in the situation itself.

BM—Most of your reservations about science seem to relate to the older mechanistic model, to the positivist view if you will. But you write a whole chapter on the emerging "new science" as holistic, favorable to participatory knowing, dynamic rather than static, non-reductionist, and so forth. If we may quote from your book, you say: "The fundamental change in modern physics has been toward a conception of the world to be conceived primarily in terms of flowing energy patterns, systemic wholeness, and mutual interaction and interdependence." Isn't this all to the good?

DS—Not entirely. I look at the new science critically and don't embrace it wholeheartedly.

BM—You embrace it more, at any rate.

DS—I think it opens up new vistas for human ways of knowing. It makes room for the view that knowledge is participative, that we can't separate the knower from the known, that knowing the world means an engagement with the world, not a detachment from it. But I also note that the new science is being interpreted in ways that could short circuit these possibilities, and this is a great danger which goes unobserved by many people.

BM—What is the problem here?

DS—To begin with, much of the new science isn't new at all. A lot of biology, for example, is straight out of the nineteenth-century mechanistic model. So the big problem is that the new science tends to be interpreted within the instrumental framework of the old science. This perspective assumes we don't know the world as such. What we have are instruments, theories, and constructs which permit us to perform intellectual operations upon whatever it is that is out there in order to get certain results—rockets, bombs, and other technological marvels. But no claim is made for the truth of what is out there. The problem here is that science has no built-in self-criticism mechanism because it determines within its own formal framework what it is it has to do. It doesn't have to ask any value questions or submit to any moral constraints, and becomes divorced from the real world of meaning, purpose, and quality.

BM—Isn't this a problem with the humanities as well? It's a truism to say that all disciplines are culture bound, that we are all enclosed in our symbolic universe.

DS—That is because the humanities have capitulated to the pre-vailing mode of scientific knowledge. They have adopted what can be called a two-realm theory of truth. On the one hand, there is the realm of knowledge provided by science. On the other, humanists think there is another realm of knowledge which is about values. But it isn't really knowledge. It is more a realm of attitudes, feelings, subjective impressions, or whatever. Thus we have two worlds which are split apart.

BM—We tend to blame science for this predicament. But couldn't it be maintained that the humanists themselves must bear a lion's share of the blame? After all, they were in the business of constructing self-sustaining formal systems before the scientists.

DS—That pushes the question back in an interesting way. I am not sure. My instinct is to say that this kind of formalism came directly out of science but that science itself came out of certain deeper movements within human consciousness. In order for science to be at all, there had to be certain dispositions of the mind, certain conceptions of the world and self, a partiality to one kind of symbolic formation over another. It's all deeply bound up with the question of of human creativity and how this manifests itself in both beneficial and destructive ways. Science, of course, grows out of human creativity. But once it is formalized into theories and methodologies, it strays from the broader context of values.

BM—An interesting word, "values." You quote the British humanist Owen Barfield to the effect that values talk is a way of avoiding any commitment to or recognition of qualities that are objectively real. Do you agree with that view?

DS—Two things we can be sure of. When people talk about values they have given up talking about reality. And, secondly, it is a kind of residual way of keeping conversation alive about certain areas that we know are very important in human life. But it's doomed.

BM—Doomed?

DS—Yes, because that which is deemed to provide knowledge will always encroach on that space we reserve for values. Until our ways of knowledge are transformed to make room for the human concerns of meaning, purpose, and quality—above all, quality—values will always be on the defensive. I agree with Barfield when he says that in the long run the head will win over the heart.

BM—What is a better word for "values"?

DS—I prefer "qualities."

BM—How do you answer the claim that the world science has created is not conspicuously worse than other worlds, people are not

less decent, societies are not less free, individual rights are better
defended than in the days when the humanists ruled the roost, that
perhaps Bacon was right and science has indeed relieved the human
estate?

DS—Well, I can agree with much of that. I have never argued that
we can go back to an earlier age, an earlier value system, nor ought
we. Modern science has made certain things possible that are absolutely necessary.

BM—Such as?

DS—I can give three examples. Freedom, as we experience it, is unquestionably partly an outcome of modern philosophy and science.
But if it is cut off from a wider matrix of meaning and community, it
becomes anarchy. Individualism is a good thing. But, cut off from a
wider matrix, it becomes atomistic and anomic. Such persons
abound in the modern world and they are ripe for being herded
together into the pseudo communities of collectivism and totalitarianism. A third example is control of nature. Control over a capri-
cious nature is also a good thing. We have now reached a point where
it seems that we have gone too far. An ecologic crisis in upon us.
Technological advance now literally threatens the future of the earth.
That is my answer to the cozy, Baconian humanist. He is looking at
one side of the situation, the good side, but not at the other, towards
which we are pretty rapidly headed. So, we can't go back.

BM—But in your book you do want to go back.

DS—No I don't.

BM—You talk about the radical humanities and about the need
for traditional wisdom. We'll come to the question of traditional
wisdom in a bit. Let's ask now what you mean by the radical
humanities?

DS—I mean those achievements of the human spirit that talk
about values as realities and not merely as useful fictions.

BM—Like what?

DS—There aren't many. Most of the humanities today are self-
enclosed systems.

BM—Why aren't useful fictions humanistic values?

DS—They would be if the claim weren't made that that is all they
are.

BM—So you are going back, then, to a conception of the humani-
ties that makes ontological claims; that is, they say real things about a
real world, provide real knowledge.

DS—I think the key is in language. The radical humanities foster respect for language and a love of words. A number of writers have pointed out the connection between the degradation of the human being and the degradation of language. The poet Wendell Berry, for one, has described the intimate relation between language and community. I believe that the increasing unreliability of language parallels the increasing disintegration of persons and communities. The capacity of words to serve as bearers of meaning is coupled with the health and meaningfulness of the personal, communal, and cosmic realities from which words spring. In a world stripped of qualities, words, too, are emptied of their substance. They are no longer capable of bearing witness to that which constitutes the innermost character of personal experience, the ultimate reality of things, and standards for beauty and responsible conduct. In a disqualified universe, the only objective meaning accorded to words is in their use as functional signs for achieving some specified pragmatic purpose. But this is an objectivity that makes no claim to be guided by the search for truth, or interest in it; it is an objectivity that has explicitly repudiated the possibility of an aesthetic, ethical, and most of all, metaphysical reference. It is a parody of what objectivity was once thought to stand for. A purely functional language is not a language for the forming of community, for the guidance of responsible conduct, or for the apprehension of mystery and vision. It is not a language for education or public discussion.

BM—And you turn to traditional models for support of the radical humanities?

DS—There is common ground between my concept of the radical humanities and a living tradition. Both speak of a kind of knowing that is more than a mere getting and having of information. Both speak of a knowing that goes beyond accumulation and manipulation to a knowing that is participation and being. Traditional wisdom is redolent of knowing that comes not from a detached looking on, but from an immediate participation in the known, a kind of indwelling in the surrounding reality of nature and the cosmos, and a knowing which is expressed through myth, symbol, and image. Traditional cultures are full of symbols that serve to sum up and convey the experience of living in a universe in which everything visible is an expression and invocation of the larger reality from which it comes. Modern culture has nearly lost this sense of the living symbol. The classical notion of the symbol as that which participates in the reality it represents has become nearly incomprehensible.

BM—This entails, as the title of your book suggests, that we must enlarge our capacities for insight and imagination.

DS—Yes. If we do this successfully we will come to realize that qualities as well as quantities are real.

BM—Not to harp a point to death, but this does take you back.

DS—To the extent that traditions are models of qualitative thinking, yes. There is no strategy of directly importing traditional values that will work. Either we end up with a two-realm-theory realm of truth, or we end up with some form of fundamentalism which rejects the achievements of the modern world. An important outcome of studying traditions is to understand that there are other ways of looking at the world and that we ought not hastily write off 99 percent of human history as mistaken.

BM—It seems a little sad that we find ourselves in this predicament to begin with. What kind of comment on our human nature is it when we construct intellectual systems like science and technology that don't do justice to our humanity?

DS—A good question. And it takes me back to my thesis about transforming our ways of knowing. All intellectual systems are in some way limiting. But a historical view suggests that we can overcome these limitations. We have not yet in our culture discovered a way of knowing that adequately combines the quantitative and the qualitative.

BM—One wonders if at bottom the distinction between quality and quantity is not a distinction without a real difference which merely hampers clear thinking. You agree that science is infused with choices, intentionality, aims, and purposes, and that many of the results of science are themselves humanistic. What precisely is your complaint?

DS—What is my complaint? Well, I think the distinction between quality and quantity is a good way to try to make that clear. I think there is a distinction and that it indeed makes a difference, but you are correct in suggesting that a complete separation between the two ought not be made. One way of getting hold of what is at stake is to recall the distinction made by Galileo at the beginning of the scientific revolution. He distinguished between primary and secondary qualities. Primary qualities like mass and motion were objective, really out there. Secondary qualities included color, sound, smell, taste, tone, form, purpose, and, by extension, life and consciousness.

These were regarded as secondary because they seemed bound up with feelings and sensations and, as such, were regarded as purely subjective and hence to be eliminated from scientific knowing. In other words, from the beginning of the scientific revolutions in both method and content, the only qualities that were permitted in science were quantitative by definition. This gave science tremendous power in dealing with the measurable and mechanical dimensions of reality. I have no complaint with that. Where trouble starts is when the further claim is made that primary qualities are all there is, that the qualitative is merely subjective and ultimately unreal. This has meant that in our dominant ways of knowing all that is most important to human beings has been left out. The qualitative dimension—especially the qualities of life, consciousness, and conscience—come also to be seen in the end as unreal, as epiphenomena of an underlying quantitative substratum that is taken to be true reality. And we get this view of things reinforced on every hand. Often, it comes to us in our textbooks and popular science as a kind of naive realism which depicts the universe as a lifeless machine or a collection of dead matter in motion. Most scientists when they are talking to each other, rather than to the public (at which time they do indulge in a good deal of naive realism), are most sophisticated and claim for themselves only an instrumental knowing that deals only with the formal aspects of numbers, motion, and force. In either case, there is no place for the qualities that make up life and conscious experience.

BM—Let's scrutinize that charge further. One still detects an ambiguity in your thinking because not only do many scientists claim to be dealing with human qualities but you agree that they do.

DS—Well, things get more complicated here. Yes, there is an ambiguity, but it is in science itself. Although it claims to deal only with the quantitative as real, science is rooted in a qualitative foundation. Many years ago, Dewey pointed out that science would be impossible without the scientist's own commitment to qualitative ideas like devotion to the truth, freedom of inquiry, personal responsibility, personal interest, attention to careful observation of phenomena, and so forth. It is from this prior commitment to qualitative reality that truly humanistic possibilities arise, but these are frustrated by a tendency to build up a view of the world that has no place for them. And here we see the real tragedy of those scientists today who are truly concerned about our most pressing human problems. Many modern scientists are in the forefront of those concerned with human values and the future of life on earth. The tragedy is that their own genuine ideals and human concerns find no support in the conceptions of knowledge and reality that dominate their own scientific method and worldview. They undercut themselves. Part of my argument in the book is that if we look seriously at the reality of the very qualities that alone make science possible and what they imply, then the needed transformation of our thinking and knowing would have to follow. We could then begin to talk about qualities as real. To use Barfield's phrase, we could begin to recognize that qualities are objective *and* subjective. We could begin to develop ways of knowing that recognize not only the limited domain of the mechanical but also the deeper and prior dimensions of meaning, life, consciousness, and conscience as equally real. But to transform our ways of knowing in this way will require a transformation of the knower, of ourselves. For how is it possible that we could begin to recognize qualities in reality without being able to bring them to birth and to recognize them within ourselves? Whether the modern world wants to go through this painful self-transformation is the intellectual-moral question of our day.

BM—Do you think the various crises we face will force us to move toward more qualitative modes of thought?

DS—If we don't we are goners.

BM—Do you find that students are becoming more concerned with these questions?

DS—There are pockets of concern. And they are growing and beginning to establish connections with one another. But I do not detect any widespread awareness. There is a lot of fear and anger. People are frustrated. They don't know how to think about complex issues. This is the great failure of education: It doesn't equip us to think creatively about real problems we face. That is why there is such a fundamentalist reaction in the country today. However simplistic, it is nonetheless understandable.

BM—That is a scary indictment of education. Why hasn't the educational community mobilized against these imminent dangers? It would seem that the question of peace and war in our time is absolutely preemptive of all other issues and that we ought to be pooling our best energies to deal with it.

DS—It's very complex. In part, it is because our ways of knowing let us down here. To deal with a problem like nuclear war we have to go outside of our customary mind set. Then the questions become

"Where do we go and what new intellectual capacities and perspectives do we develop?" If we look upon the world as a machine, as most scientists encourage us to do, we can adopt some very callous attitudes. We can say things like, "All machines run down, why not the planet earth?" Robert Jay Lifton says this is the most prevalent form of cynicism in academe. Time and time again his colleagues have told him that every species becomes extinct so why not the human species? This attitude stems directly from the reductionist views science inculcates.

BM—This might indicate more the exhaustion of the paradigm than the end of the human race.

DS—That is entirely possible. I do think the paradigms are breaking down. We have to re-educate ourselves.

BM—Where will the creative thrust in this direction come from? Do we have to wait, as the philosopher Martin Heidegger says, for a new god to be born? Will it come from schools of education, colleges, universities?

DS—No, not from these sources. They are too much a part of the problem. I think that in order to change educational structures we have, among other things, to begin with the child and how the child comes to know. That is why the last chapter of my book concentrates on the education of children. There I draw upon the Waldorf experiment in education to argue that the education of the child involves willing, feeling, and sensing. All three! Before we can reform educational structures we have to reexamine what is involved in the knowing process, and this takes us back to the child. Curriculum reform must begin at that level.

BM—Most Americans are not familiar with the Waldorf schools.

DS—No, and this is not surprising as far as most Americans are concerned. However, it is shocking that so few American professional educationists know little if anything about them. Waldorf education is over sixty years old and constitutes one of the largest, if not the largest, independent school movements in the world with some three hundred schools.

BM—Where did the movement begin?

DS—In Germany in 1919 under the direct influence of the remarkable philosopher-educator Rudolph Steiner. Steiner was interested in developing a way of knowing rooted in the total human being, and the results of his work have flowed into many areas besides education, such as agriculture, medicine, art, science, and social renewal.

BM—What was Steiner's basic philosophy?

DS—He made three main contributions. First, an understanding of knowing that enhances thinking, feeling, and willing. Second, a detailed account of child development, which has been confirmed and extended by developmental psychologists. Third, a rich and detailed curriculum and pedagogical approach unique in modern education.

BM—Your book appears to reflect a good deal of Steiner's philosophy.

DS—Absolutely. He was the major influence on my theory of educating the imagination.

BM—One of the best parts of your book is the thorough and very sensitive way in which you develop a rich theory of the imagination. Do you mean by imagination something like the fuller rationality exemplified in older traditions? Or is it something different?

DS—I think it is something different. I am really trying to re-establish a fuller notion of the imagination. We have narrowed the meaning of rationality in our culture, and likewise we have narrowed the meaning of the imagination. It tends to connote something purely fictive, basically unreal, and trivial. I borrow from Owen Barfield to talk about imagination as the activity of the whole person. Knowing involves thinking, willing, feeling, valuing, and doing. This total involvement of the whole person is the act of the imagination. To the extent that traditional rationality embraced this wholeness, I suppose we could say that by imagination I mean this fuller rationality, but one that must be exercised in the distinct circumstances of our modern life. I stand pat by my claim that consciousness evolves.

An adequate conception of education, an education of imagination, will always strive for that way of knowing which springs from the participation of the person as a total willing, feeling, valuing, thinking being—a way of knowing that leads to the wisdom in living that makes personal life truly possible and worthy. It will have as its prime purpose, as its ground and aim, the complete, harmonious realization of the full capacities and potential of the individual as a whole person. Any conception of education that arises from some other or lesser concern or that fastens on a partial or isolated aspect of the total person will finally abort, delivering only fragments of persons and figments in place of reality. And by its nature, such a lesser education cannot avoid serving purposes that will be basically non-human and ultimately inhuman.

BM—Where do you think educators got off the track?

DS—Contemporary education, in theory and practice, has moved steadily away from conceptions of knowing as involving the participation, harmonizing, and liberation of the whole person. The majority of leading educational theorists, and those parents, teachers, and educational agencies most in touch with the forefront of educational research, are bent chiefly on developing the academic brightness of the students. The literature of educational research is rife with talk about "stages of intellectual development," "academic readiness," "the extension and enhancement of the learner's cognitive structures," and so forth. Deeply concerned parents fret whether they have yet done enough to promote the academic readiness of their two-year-old; caring teachers strive to create situations conducive to proper "cognitive growth"; educational researchers are indefatigable in their efforts to discern the earliest traces in young brains of evolving "cognitive structures and conceptual networks" and to establish the "optimal conditions" for them. In all of this there is a good deal of idealism and deeply felt commitment.

BM—Most people would say the emphasis on cognition is good. Isn't that what back to basics is all about?

DS—At first glance, the contemporary emphasis on cognition would seem to be the proper aim of education and to be welcomed by anyone concerned with our ways of knowing. A closer look, however, begins to reveal that at almost every point in modern education the meaning of cognition is exceedingly narrow and limited. Cognition turns out to mean almost exclusively verbal and logical mathematical skills (often measured by IQ tests). Cognition is narrowly conceived as a matter of discursive knowledge and calculative intellect, and the essence of education is accordingly taken to consist entirely in the imparting and retention of information and the development of logical-mathematical facility. In other words, the narrowing of reason to mean only discursive and technical reason has taken root in the heart of modern education, and has been written into the assumptions of educational research, educational administration, and classroom and family teaching. The results of this narrowing of reason, here, as elsewhere, have been devastating.

BM—Can you be specific about these devastating results?

DS—One result has been a tendency within education to value children and youth not as persons in their own right and with their own inherent value, but only as potential learners. The problem would not be as serious if learning in turn were not conceived in its most restricted sense as being solely the development of calculative skills and the acquisition of subject matter. A premium is placed on narrow intellectual attributes, while other capacities and aptitudes, personal, social, moral, aesthetic, go unattended. The deep wisdom inherent in the body and in the emotions is neglected. Instead, the natural energies and passions of the child become problems to be dealt with. Discipline then becomes something imposed from without to hold the emotions under control and to contain them. Or in more progressive-minded classrooms, the emotions may be used to catch the students' interest, to lure them to the lesson at hand, a kind of candy coating on the bitter pill of learning. In either case, the potential for knowing and the wisdom already at work in the whole person are not valued and frequently go unperceived. Aptitudes and qualities in the child essential to a meaningful, satisfying, full, and competent life are overlooked and suppressed.

Another result of an education tied mainly to the enhancement of mental facility measured by academic achievement is that it reflects and furthers the steady deterioration of the resources necessary for significant cultural criticism and renewal. Put more bluntly, if carried out consistently, it leads to a cultural desert. This is not to say that every experience in modern education is utterly bleak and without social value, for there are many persons at work, teachers, parents, and others, concerned to make education a force for social and cultural renewal. And their efforts, and often successes, need to be recognized and affirmed. The point is, however, that there is very little in the underlying assumptions of current educational theory and practice to lend support to such efforts, and a good deal that directly undercuts them.

BM—What values should a good education inculcate?

DS—An education that stresses only narrow mental facility offers no foundation for resisting and stemming the relentless contemporary erosion of the communal forces essential to cultural health. A sense of time and place; the cultivation of mutuality; a sense of natural rhythm; celebratory traditions of communal renewal and hope; the pride and beauty of craft; vocation experienced as a genuine summons or calling, *vocatio*, in which the challenge of the task, pride in one's work, and the satisfaction of serving actual human needs are central; a deeply felt, because deeply real, sense of civic responsibility—all that which makes for the sources of significance and cultural richness necessary to a free and vital society is constantly uprooted and dissolved away where an abstract rationality and technical reason dominate.

BM—Amplify what you mean by civic responsibility.

DS—An exclusive emphasis on the development of instrumental, technical reason reduces rationality to a consideration only of quantities and quantitative relationships, which in the public sphere means a preoccupation with the lowest common denominator, material elements of society, and with their manipulation, management, and control. The result is to strip public deliberations of all cultural contents and to cripple the capacity of the public and its leaders to deal with the qualitative dimensions of public life. The ensuing cultural improverishment becomes manifest at nearly every point in the society, especially in the realm of international affairs. □

An Interview with
MANFRED STANLEY on

Taming the Technocratic Ego

IN ancient Rome, the temple of Janus ran east and west to symbolize
the hope of dawn and the day's ending at sunset. In his two faces were
inscribed the mysteries of time itself: youth and age, life and death,
permanence and change.

In our society, technology plays a Janus-like role as the focus of
our highest hopes and our worst fears. For it is a fact that a great
many of our anxieties and frustrations stem from the technology we
have created. Our technological creations threaten our freedom, they
often make our lives complicated and unpleasant, they are difficult to
control, and, above all, they have the awesome power to destroy life
itself and, indeed, the very planet we inhabit. Not surprisingly,
technology has taken on a spectral aspect in much contemporary
literature. It appears as a congeries of vast, impersonal, and very
powerful forces which become embedded in our psyches and generate in us feelings of impotence and repressed terror.

The technophobes have two compelling arguments on their side.
First, technology does introduce change, constant and rapid, in such
ways that the social context in which we attempt to define the public
is sytematically destabilized. Second, disclosure about the public is
more and more determined by technological considerations rather

than political or ethical values. Think, for example, of how technology creates a Babel of specialized languages and thus abets the private over the public. Our traditional categories are inadequate to a discussion of such large-scale problems as nuclear war, the impact of technology on the environment, or the effects of genetic research on future generations. Our available concepts and the new problems generated by technology are at some distance from one another.

It is a safe generalization to say that the greatest transformations in American society since the founders have been brought about by technology—by science, to be sure, but science as it is embodied in powerful technological forms.

One of the best commentators on this complex subject I know is Manfred Stanley. His book *The Technological Conscience: Survival and Dignity in an Age of Expertise* remains among the finest in a fast field. Shortly after it appeared, I flew to Syracuse on a winter's day when the snows were high and the sun was bright for what turned out to be the first of many talks with Stanley, who is professor of sociology at Syracuse University and director of the Center for the Study of Citizenship.

"I am concerned with technology," he told me, "and I am concerned with education. And these two concerns come together in my concern with citizenship. At our center we have formulated five basic questions. One, do classical civic concepts such as public, polity, office, civic virtue, and citizenship have any relevance in a modern political culture based on the ideas of interest group, pluralism, cost-benefit, and public policy? Two, can expert authority be reconciled with popular sovereignty? Three, how do the theoretical concerns of the social sciences and philosophy relate to civic issues? Four, what is a non-technocratic, civic concept of public policy? And, five, is civic education possible?

I asked Stanley how it came about that his thinking came to focus on citizenship. He digressed to talk about his early years as a refugee from Nazism.

"I came to America when I was five," he said, "and my earliest memory was a sense of safety that only those who flee can know. Two other memories stand out. One is of New York City. I do not refer to what a sober demographer or economist would have in mind. I mean the city as an object of love, joy, aspiration, and commitment. In my mythic imagination, New York was at once a socialist utopia of public institutions and a modern Athens of myriad forums (little magazines, youth groups of every variety, colleges and universities, town halls, and union squares), cosmopolis in human scale. Walking its streets, attending its schools, washing dishes in its hot dog stands, working odd jobs in its warehouses, doing social work among its suffering, my belief that New York is America remained unshaken until I left it for good in that emigration which only the wealthy, the poor, or the obsessed were spared."

Stanley recalled two movies from his American childhood. "One, the first I ever saw in this country, was *Pride of the Yankees*. The story of a shy youngster who became great, the movie dramatized for me the myth of America: the balance between community and individual, between the romanticism of humility and possibility of achievement. In my mind, baseball and democracy are fused, and the old New York Yankees still epitomize some benign version of aristocracy and tradition whose mysteries even cynics never quite adequately explain to me as bombast and money. Lou Gehrig is not a bad introduction to hero worship in a democracy.

"The second movie I saw in America was the film version of H. G. Wells's novel *The Shape of Things to Come*. A visual hymn of technocratic scientism, this film engraved on my imagination the dramaturgical structure of all my subsequent professional preoccupations, in both theory and practice. The definitive war it depicts (so close, then, over the horizon) and the imagery of salvation and rebirth through technological reconstruction of the world overwhelmed me with what only a mature, scholarly mind would later recognize as an idyllic, unworldly dream of reason. These early experiences provided the myth line of my life: refuge, liberation, technology, reconstruction."

I wondered if there was a connection between the Wells novel and *The Technological Conscience*. This prompted my first question.

BM—Why did you write the book?
MS—It was partly a response to the 1960s, but in a particular way. The counterculture was a strong reaction against the whole tradition of reason in the West. A book like Theodore Roszak's *The Making of a Counter Culture*, for example, typified for me what was wrong with that whole approach. It was a primitivist rejection of the project of civilization. I had a close relationship with the late Benjamin Nelson, that remarkable intellectual historian of medieval thought and soci-

ologist of modern culture. His concern for the integrity and the tenuousness of Western evolving standards of reason in law, science and morality influenced my reaction to the primitivist romanticism of the sixties. Also, I spent a year as research associate with the Harvard University Program on Technology and Society in 1970, plus part time thereafter until its demise. The program's director, Emmanuel Mesthene, challenged me directly to write this book by saying he could not understand what people like Herbert Marcuse and Jacques Ellul were up to. He suspected that they were just irrational.

BM—But you didn't think they were irrational?

MS—No. They confronted me with the problem of technology as it had previously been raised in Germany. Since I am a refugee from Nazism, I was particularly sensitive to that discourse. The book had a lot to do with what I thought of as the implications of personal history. Was Nazism a price we paid for technological mindlessness? Was it somehow the triumph or the rejection of an alleged technological worldview? Americans can afford to be complacent about such issues because twentieth-century history hasn't happened on the North American continent yet in some important ways. What I felt I had to do was assimilate the arguments of the critics of technology into the mainstream of American sociological thought. But I had to do it in such a way as not to join the primitivist wing of that critique against science and technology as such. I saw myself as trying to help renovate the whole project of Western rationality.

BM—But you are walking a tightrope there. On the one hand, you want to disassociate yourself from the counterculturalists, but you yourself are a counterculturalist, of a sort. You are criticizing much the same thing they were.

MS—But I tried to do it in such a way as not to make a demonology out of my criticism.

BM—Your book depends on a basic distinction between technology and what you call technicism. Technology, as the application of reason to problem solving, is legitimate. But technicism is the illegitimate extension of technological modes of thought to cultural, moral, and political thinking. You say technicism is "the reconstitution of the world as a problem-solving system." How real is that distinction? Doesn't technology lead inevitably to technicism?

MS—No. That would be technological determinism, which I reject.

BM—You wouldn't agree with Ellul then?

MS—No. Probably the most critical pressure I have had is from my Marxist friends. They charge that my book is an indulgent exercise in philosophical idealism. They think that I have made the technological problem too much of a linguistic problem, as though symbolic formulations were determinative of the social order rather than the underlying economic order which generates interest groups who profit from the sort of mystifications I was attacking.

BM—What exactly do you mean by mystification?

MS—Well, that's difficult to be brief about; a lot of my book is about that question. Let's for the moment just say that mystification is the failure to apply current standards of critical reason (whatever these may be at any given historical moment) to those issues which we have a stake in being vague about. Mystification especially occurs when this vagueness is transformed into pseudo-clarity by means of linguistic shortcuts like the fallacy of misplaced concreteness.

BM—Would you agree that technology is the cutting edge of creativity in our society?

MS—It would be simply foolish of me not to answer yes to that question, whatever qualifications I would want to add. However, there are a number of ways to answer yes to that question. One could answer yes by pointing out that whenever we read about a bright, precocious kid in the newspapers, he is always billed as a future MIT student, destined to study math and science and computer engineering. It is true that our best talent is attracted to technology, whereas in another age it might have been religion or art or politics. Another way of answering yes to that question is to note that technology, including social technologies like bureaucracies, are altering the entire moral and political shape of the world and creating systemic structures of global proportions which contradict the traditional moral and political boundaries. This is not an original thought, but a fact nonetheless. Thirdly, technology is the one undisputed shared interest of all our major institutions. Everybody, rightly or wrongly, believes that investment in technology is what we most need now. I think this is a very unexamined belief, but it is another way in which technology is the cutting edge. And there is a more positive way in which technology is a cutting edge, one that I feel strongly about. Technology could, in fact, help us solve monumental problems. If you pressed me on the question of what is wrong with technology, I would say, it is not technology, but the uses to which it is put.

BM—In other words, technicism. But that raises again the force of the distinction. If technology (or technicism) fills up all of our cultural and psychic space, then how do we gain some critical purchase outside of it? The haunting question becomes: Are there effective generators of ideas and attitudes in their own right? Ellul, for example, argues that there are no such spheres. In your book, you don't actually say there are other spheres. You argue that there should be. But do they exist?

MS—I think we have to explore what we mean by "spheres" in this context. We might mean, for example, a public forum, which is to say a context of speech that is not dominated by technological imagery. Or we might mean spheres of action in which people can act out destinies not dominated by their position in systems of technology. Here is where my Marxist friends have a real point to make. They would say that the dominant sphere is not technology but the corporate economy.

BM—But the corporate economy is just another form of technology.

MS—Yes and no. The Marxist position is that the corporations decide how technology will be used. And in whose interests. Take a specific example. In *America by Design*, David Noble shows with a wealth of historical detail that the American engineering profession could have been very different from what it turned out to be. The reason it is the way it is can be attributed to the fact that at the very beginning there was a convergence between the corporate management of science-based industry and the incipient engineering profession. That convergence resulted in a career line that featured vast numbers of engineers becoming corporate managers. The emergence of university industrial engineering and corporate management programs thus was not due to technology as an independent causal force but was rather an example of how technology was a dependent variable of a more independent causal factor which was the corporate organization of industry.

BM—Isn't this what the Marxists call ideology?

MS—They would say that what I call technicism is ideology.

BM—Did you write the book from a basically Marxist perspective?

MS—No. I wanted to reach audiences that cross ideological boundaries. One of the things I think is terribly wrong in our times is that so much discussion is preempted by ideological partisanship. Terms like left and right, and all the isms we use, are increasingly irrelevant. I think there are many serious people now who are worried about what we loosely call Western civilization and worry about it in different ideological idioms. They need to come together on the basis of their seriousness and the substance of what they may care about rather than their ideological origins.

BM—And this basis is, for you, language. The major contention of your book is that education is linguistic competence, or a standard of literacy appropriate to a community of persons. To be literate, you say on page 221 of your book, "is to attend to the world around us; to interpret what we see and hear; to name in our voices the conclusions we are prepared to let inform our conduct." For you, language is a form of human agency, a form of community, a form of consciousness, an instrument of world creation. Through language, we become responsible moral participants in "the community of language." You attribute an almost magical power to language. Has anybody pointed that out?

MS—I have been influenced by certain trends in the sociology of language that have themselves been influenced by philosophy going back to Wittgenstein—the notion of language as a form of life. The idea here is to bring language back into the world as a mode of action. I recognize that one criticism that might be made of me is that, whatever I may think, I write as if language is all there is. It may be the bias of an educator. We are, after all, perhaps the only group in society whose professional conscience demands a nonmanipulative, even nonutilitarian attitude toward language. This may be a purist position. But it includes the study of language as an aspect of action. I think our education lacks an objective focus on that dimension of languages. Most especially, we fail to examine with our students the moral implication of using technical vocabularies in place of political vocabularies. And so, in my work, I come down hard on that problem.

BM—There is a Platonic flavor here. To know the good is to do the good. Some would object that knowing and doing are two different categories. But the comeback is to say that knowing is already a form of doing, and thus dissolve the distinction. But if we pursue this line too far we are apt to land in a philosophical squirrel cage.

MS—It's a difficult problem. Hannah Arendt struggled with it in the last years of her life.

BM—Did you know ner?

MS—Not personally. But as you might imagine, she was one of my mentors. I'm teaching a course this fall entitled The Sociology of Evil, in which I wrestle with some of these questions. By the way, did you get the impression from my book that I have a kind of conspiracy theory in these matters?

BM—One could.

MS—Let me put it on the record that I did not intend a conspiracy theory and would very much regret having my book interpreted that way.

BM—But you seem to detect behind every social process some form of mystification.

MS—That is always true. It's just part of the human condition. The educational task is always one of demystification, no matter what social order we live in—to establish that critical distance that prevents us from becoming unwitting handmaidens to any structure of authority. But is is important to distinguish demystification from debunking.

BM—What is the difference?

MS—In my book I make use of an important article by Albert Borgmann on device paradigms in which he develops a phenomenology of concealment through technology. His analysis fits in well with the critique of black box imagery. What I mean by mystification is inappropriate recourse to black box thinking. Now, black box thinking is an ordinary feature of the human mind. We always do it unconsciously. But one of the things we have learned in the philosophy of language and cognitive psychology in the twentieth century is the dynamics of black box cognitive mechanisms. We have become reflexively conscious of how we use such mechanisms in thinking, in explaining, in talking. The project of demystification is not one of debunking so that truth with a capital T can emerge; rather it is extreme reflexiveness, extreme self-awareness on how one uses black boxes to get around difficult problems in such a way as to relieve us of responsibility for our actions. Black boxes are related to what Walter Lippmann meant by stereotyping. Demystification is criticism of such morally questionable recourses. Then the question becomes, how do you know when something is morally illegitimate? Generally speaking, anything that compromises human dignity is immoral. That is why I spend a lot of time in the book working out a concept of human dignity relevant to this issue, and I then ask: What does human dignity have to do with language? And the answer, of course, is, a great deal, and I go to some length to demonstrate how. Debunking is when we stand on Mount Olympus and say: I can see farther than you. Debunking is cheap demystification.

BM—There still seems to be a problem. If through language we participate in the creation of new symbolic forms that eventually come to dominate our collective consciousness, then don't we encounter yet another form of mystification? Isn't it true that what dominates also mystifies?

MS—Critical thinking has always to set itself against whatever form of domination we encounter. Each new pattern of domination releases a new wave of challenges for critical thought.

BM—How do you think we are being mystified today?

MS—I am impressed by the recent revisionist literature inspired by Quentin Skinner on early modern political philosophy which illustrates how concerned our recent ancestors (including Adam Smith) still were with the integrity of classical political ideas (e.g., republican virtue, citizen participation, civic bonds, etc.). Since then, and fully by now, we have allowed the economists to capture the official language of the social order. I see the effects of this all over the place. The fragmentation of the educational community, for example, is something that we educators have allowed to happen, and the only reconciling language we seem to tolerate is that of the market. Technology and economics generate today the most potent mystifications. There isn't time to go into this here at length. But I'm struck by the continuities between the mystifications of economics and technology. The idea of a self-regulating market is related in some ways to the notion of a self-regulating problem-solving system of the sort envisioned in a society as a cybernetic system. In their common emphasis on natural system dynamics, both images downgrade the polity as a voluntary deliberative community of citizens.

BM—You write that "as listeners we reside in a fully human world."

MS—As listeners, yes.

BM—Unless you want to say that we hear the voice of nature or the voice of God or whatever.

MS—I wouldn't want to say that.

BM—But you do want to say that language is the primary form of human consciousness?

MS—For the purpose of this book at least. You asked earlier why I wrote the book. Let me return to that question here in a way that may clarify this present portion of our discussion. For anyone of my generation, the question of where we stand on revolution is a very serious matter. There seem to me really only three ways we can think of problem solving. One is through authority in the manner of the Grand Inquisitor. A second way is revolution. And the third is education. Authority has to do with control; it utilizes mystery and music and magic to reconcile the human soul with whatever those in authority regard as the human condition. Revolution is basically rooted in the view that everything that is wrong with the human condition is wrong because of the way the social structure is organized. Education is based on the view that there is enough that is redemptive about the way a society is organized that one still has time to talk about human character. This is a legitimate kind of idealism, I think. My book is not about revolution. It is a critique of authority, especially as mystified by technicist vocabularies, and a vote of confidence in education.

BM—Why is revolution so important a subject for intellectuals? They seem to need it least and are usually the first to go to the wall when it comes.

MS—Because we are not just intellectuals. We are thinkers for others, representatives of the polity. We also think as citizens. There are certain issues for which we are responsible, in the sense that not to have a judgment about certain critical questions is to be irresponsible. One of these questions is revolution. Let me make myself clear: I feel as did Hannah Arendt that revolution must be ruled out now for those of us living in the industrialized countries of the West. The revolutions of communism and facism have wreaked havoc. A revolution in the United States would lead to catastrophe. I am even against a constitutional convention because I think it would compromise the Bill of Rights. But most of the world does not enjoy the freedoms we do; most of the world lives in oppression; most of the world feels ripe for revolution.

BM—How do you know when there is a need for revolution?

MS—When human dignity is intolerably oppressed, and we are each responsible for having a credible view of what we mean by intolerable that we are prepared to debate in the public forum.

BM—Let's go back to something you said about the economists preempting all the controlling metaphors of society. What would you say to someone like Daniel Bell, who argues that the social system in the United States is made up of three quite independent systems of institutions organized along different axes and with different values? He calls these a political system, an economic system, and a moral-cultural system. Aren't there many voices in America? Isn't this what we mean by pluralism?

MS—Good question. Let me address the issue of pluralism in this way. I grant that there are multiple voices in our society. That is clearly true. The next question is: Which of these voices are more powerful and why? If you ask which institutions give power—not just authority, but power—to voices, then the focus of the question changes. What concerns me is not the multiplicity of voices but the institutions that lie behind them. Take Bell's taxonomy. The moral-cultural realm goes back at least two thousand years. Bell is quite right to say there has come about a disassociation between our culture and our society in the sense that most of our moral-cultural language was generated in pre-modern societies that could be located on another planet as far as what our society today looks like. We all recognize that.

BM—And the polity?

MS—Let me be blunt. I will make the point perhaps more forcefully than I believe it. Let me say that I think the polity is dead. I don't think there is a polity. The language of the polity has been almost totally taken over by the language of the economy. Expressions like consumer sovereignty, the use of political advertising techniques, the cross-over of leaders from private industry to government (as though experience in meeeting a payroll was somehow a prerequisite for being a statesman) are indicators that the real world is the economy. The language of the market is dominant. Interest group liberalism is, to my way of thinking, an economic point of view.

BM—Your view is a widely shared one. How far do you want to push, though? You surely don't mean the polity is literally dead?

MS—In the classical sense, yes, it's dead. When I look at the different senses of the world "public" in contemporary usage, I cannot find a classically resonant sense of citizens. Nobody knows anymore what we mean by citizenship except as lobbies and lever pullers.

BM—How do you respond to the objection that the classical model won't work in a modern, democratic, heterogeneous society?

MS—That is emerging for me as the organizing question of my

entire intellectual career!
BM—Now we've struck gold.
MS—When I teach the intellectual history of sociology, I make my students begin with Aristotle's *Politics*. I also give them a lot by the Saint Simonians because they posed your argument the most clearly in its modern form.
BM—What argument?
MS—That modern industrial civilization was going to have to have its own moral culture. Emile Durkheim, one of modern sociology's greatest founders, was himself a product of this Saint Simonist consciousness of the discontinuities between classical political thought and modern societal conditions. His book on moral education is very acute in its conception of what this all means for education, although I disagree with his prescriptive views. Condorcet, Rousseau, Comte, Max Weber, Karl Mannheim, and so forth—all of these have laid out for us, their heirs, philosophically relevant questions about the reconciliation of our moral cultural heritage with modern forms of society. They helped create the sociological perspective as a dimension of liberal arts education. Modern education is impotent in any but a technocratic sense without the resources of this perspective.
BM—What about Marx?
MS—Naturally he is a major figure in that group, without question. I would only add that the tragic failure of Marx's prescriptive thought is of almost unspeakably depressing consequence for our own generation's prescriptive imagination. We have all suffered a failure of nerve in the West. Our "conservative" leaders preach Herbert Spencer to us; our moralists are nostalgic; and our visionaries make science fiction movies. The moral tragedy of Marxism has been fateful for us all. America might be a great nation, not just a world-power, if she could base her policies on a reasoned and sober analysis of this tragedy rather than just treating the whole issue as a form of demonology and world politics as a Manichean drama.
BM—Eva Braun dealt at length with some of your educational concerns in her Paradoxes of Education in a Republic.
MS—An important book, but unfortunatley written with an anti-sociological attitude that makes it difficult for her to account for what went wrong with education.
BM—Is anybody in the mainstream of sociology today interested in these questions as you see them?

MS—Some are, but often in a haphazard sort of way. Among sociologists, Habermas, Dahrendorf, and Luhman—all German sociologists—strike me as among the most innovative contributors to issues like these today. I could think of more, of course, including Americans. But in general, American mainstream sociology doesn't concern itself as explicitly as I would like with traffic between political philosophy and social science.

BM—So you are a staunch believer in a liberal education in the sense of a classical education.

MS—Yes, but in a rather offensive manner. I object, for example, to the great books approach as at St. John's of Annapolis. I see that approach as what I can only call guarding the sacred gonads. I don't think we should treat classical texts as though they were icons or sacred liturgy, fit only for endless exegetical commentary by master specialists. These texts need to be taken into the world. People need to be prodded with them; to be told: You must know this and here is why you must; these are the texts of our civilization, and they were written in passion and desire for worldly relevance.

BM—Are you saying that when the social sciences lose their roots in the classical tradition they become technicist?

MS—Exactly.

BM—Are you optimistic about our chances of reconciling the past and the present?

MS—Well, I am not pessimistic with a capital P. I know the limited relevance of the past because to think about education today is to think about something genuinely new. We can't pine for a pristine age when things were done right. The classical models of education can't help us directly in a modern democratic society.

BM—What is their chief value then?

MS—They teach us what is possible to do in the way of instilling erudition; they have produced some great teachers; they pose questions about the relationship between education and society; they show us where our ideals come from. So we can learn much from them, not least of all by asking what they did not seek to do and what they did, and what is left that we must do for ourselves.

BM—To get back to the polity question, how do you see the relevance of classical notions of the polity to our modern predicament?

MS—The notion of the classical public is a notion of identity in which we are to each other more than what divides us. It is the ultimate secular meaning of community, responsibility, and interdependence between generations.

BM—And this requires being educated in the sense of being linguistically competent?

MS—Yes. And this brings us to the distinction between school and an educative environment. In my book, I distinguish education from socialization, training, indoctrination, and schooling. Socialization refers to the ways in which the young are inducted as members of a society. Training aims to transmit specific skills; it is based upon expertise. Indoctrination seeks to inculcate students with an existing set of beliefs. Schooling is an activity whose end is the transmission of knowledge in the form of thought modules called curricula. All of these have as their purpose the reproduction in the individual of something. Education connotes for me a process which transcends these reproductive functions. Education in this sense has to do with what only the classical writers had a language for talking about. Sociologists talk about socialization too much as a reproduction of society within the psyche. It is only the classical writers who raise the question, what does it mean to intervene in one's own socialization, and to take responsibility for its vectors and tendencies? That is the question of education.

BM—And you deny we have education in this sense.

MS—Yes. I don't think we can have it under present circumstances, the circumstance of the division of labor in the university conspicuous among these. That doesn't mean, of course, that we don't find it in some classrooms.

BM—The classics seemed to convey a sense of freedom apart from, or beyond institutions, wouldn't you agree?

MS—That is an important question for sociologists because it implies that real freedom, real progress and autonomy, is to be found in the interstices of institutions rather than at the center of them. I would prefer not to believe this, but let me hear where you're going with the question.

BM—Couldn't we define democratic institutions as those that are so structured as not to commandeer what one can freely do within them, through them, above and around them?

MS—Yes, we could. But I would prefer not to leave our concept of democracy at that; it is too negative a definition of freedom for my personal taste. But go on with your line of questioning.

BM—Would you also agree that educational institutions, like all institutions, tend to corrupt the very values they promote?

MS—Corruption is connected to the lack of participation in society. My point is that very few people now participate creatively in society. You and I, for example, do not control the destiny of money. How then can we participate creatively in the economy?

BM—We make a bit of it.

MS—A small bit. I once had a student who came from a very wealthy family. He said something in class one day which I have never forgotten. He said if you have fifty thousand dollars in the bank you might be deluded into thinking that you are autonomous. If you have five hundred thousand you might think you are part of the ruling class. But if you have a million you begin to realize how little power you have. Interesting. Most of us don't make enough money to claim any power or creativity in this regard, any more than the serf in the Middle Ages was connected to the creative center of his society.

BM—But there is an argument that even the lowly serf was connected, through a complex network of liturgies, art, and political practices.

MS—That is the philosophy of consumerism writ large. He who consumes any part of his society, material or spiritual, participates in it by definition.

BM—Think of consumerism as a way in which technological man fictionalizes his experience, plugs in, as it were, to the creative goings on.

MS—It is fascinating to me that people could take this view seriously.

BM—Why do you think it so wrong-headed?

MS—I think here I'll have to resort to my use of the classical public as a model for talking about these matters. I go back to that aspect which talks about citizenship as a participatory, city-making phenomenon. This theme runs from Aristotle through Renaissance, civic humanist, English commonwealth, early American Puritan, and antifederalist thought, and is present in some ways even in the utilitarianism of John Stuart Mill. When Adam Smith and his contemporaries debated about the British public debt, what was at issue? It wasn't merely a utilitarian economic matter for them. Smith and others worried about whether a large public debt would give power to people who had little stake in the polity and that, as a result, the sense of the public and the operative virtues of citizenship would be weakened. That political way of posing an economic question is evidence of a time when questions were still intellectually evaluated to some extent in light of their effect on the moral condition of the polity. The way Jefferson felt about land would be another example from our own history. We don't talk like that anymore. Politics today is little more than economic blackmail: competitive bidding between communities, states, regions, and even nations for the support of large corporations.

BM—You sound a little alarmist at the moment.

MS—I am alarmist about our historical amnesia, about how Western political traditions are being held ransom, about education's complicity in this process.

BM—It is now time for a final question. In your book you write, in one of your more striking lines, that "the evolution of creative and responsible power over language among the democratic polities is the next great challenge of moral progress." How, at the present time, do we stand with respect to that challenge?

MS—I recognize how easily a statement like that can be reduced to the contemporary psychobabble theory that all would be well if people would just learn to communicate—the touchy-feely of the mind. I do not mean this, although, of course, there is a serious dimension to this communication hypothesis which I would not wish to demean.

In my statement, I have in mind three related generalizations. The first is that the technical complexity, moral pluralism, and social stratigraphy of modern life generate unavoidable mystifications. Second, there are genuinely new lessons being learned in our century about the creative and destructive powers of human symbolic activity. These lessons come to us from many sources: the Lippmanns and Wittgensteins of language scholarship, the psychoanalytic explorers of the inner realm, the propaganda ministries of totalitarianism, the field studies of sociologists, and the hermeneutic sensitivity of revisionist historiographers. These lessons show us to ourselves less as rational engineers of progress than as products of reflex, magic, and dreams. Third, all this adds up to a growing recognition that symbolic activity as such can be a political issue even in a democracy, an ancient insight with newly grim elaborations.

These generalizations have played havoc with our simple faith in the benefits of literacy. But further, these generalizations also prepare us to inquire more wisely into several revelations of twentieth-century life which our Enlightenment faith has seduced us into regarding as bizarre paradoxes. High culture can co-exist with unspeakable evil within the same nation and even within a single soul. Fantastically complex technologies can co-exist with almost sub-human mindlessness. Great ideals can become so abstract as to generate forms of worldly incompetence that seem almost exclusive to people with compassionate hearts. My statement, then, is meant to restore language and its uses to the status of a political philosophic issue. I am prepared to argue that linguistic inability to articulate the conceptual possibilities and limits of the market metaphor is a form of functional illiteracy every bit as politically significant as the inability to read and write.

BM—So how do we solve the problem of political agency?

MS—We don't really know under modern conditions what it means to be citizens in anything that resembles the concrete sense that our forbears from Athens to Philadelphia thought they knew. To say we do not know is one thing; to add that we can never know is quite another. It is this latter thesis that I deny. If I affirmed it, I could not in good conscience call myself a democrat any longer, certainly in any Anglo-American sense I value. The reconciliation of the calling of citizenship with the perplexities of modern conditions is an awesomely complex agenda. You and I will not see it achieved in our lifetime. Our best hope is to look to the slow refinements of scholarship and the patient courage of those who persist in practicing the arts of the public forum.

BM—Thank you. ☐

An Afterward by
BERNARD MURCHLAND

The Case for the Core

To be educated is to know that we are
worthy of our ancestors—Polybius

I WANT to argue briefly that many of the problems that beset
American higher education could be set right by adopting a core
curriculum. I define a core quite loosely as any body of classical
readings. I do not want to commit to any specific readings; nor do I
want to commit to any specific time period or discipline or culture.
What I mean by "classic" is sometimes rather archly referred to as a
"canon." I do not much like that word, but if I were to use it, it would
be in the loose sense indicated—an elastic, trans-disciplinary, multicultural concept. There are modern as well as traditional classics;
Eastern classics as well as Western ones; classics in science and the
social sciences as well as in the humanities. Because my notion of a
classic is an open one, I do not wish to be dogmatic about this or that
list. Nor am I arguing against other kinds of education. There is a
place in the sun for career education, majors, enriched and otherwise,
remedial work, and so forth. I contend only that a classical core of
some sort is necessary to any kind of education. My argument runs
on three threads.

The first might be called an epistemological argument, because it
has to do with what we learn and how we learn it; it has to do at

bottom with how we acquire truth and what is the nature of the truth we acquire. My premise here is that most of what the human race has learned is embodied in the classics. To learn means in a most basic sense becoming familiar with that body of knowledge, or some significant part of it. New knowledge is always based on old knowledge. As William James put it, "truth is largely made out of previous truths." He viewed the classics as the "funded" experience of the race, and used a horticultural image to describe the learning process. New ideas, he said, are "grafted" onto old ideas in a slow organic process that has implications for teaching, for our understanding of culture, and for the value we place upon the successor generation. E. F. Schumacher makes the same point in different words. The kinds of ideas that fill our minds, he says, determine the quality of experience. If our ideas are "small, weak, superficial, and incoherent, then life will appear insipid, uninteresting, petty, and chaotic." If our ideas do not have taproots in what mankind has thought, as opposed to what mankind presently thinks or will think, unless, in my terminology, they are rooted in a classical core, we have no basis upon which to build new knowledge and, even worse, no context for making sense of that knowledge.

Science has perhaps misled us by not being interested in its own history, thus creating a general impression that history as such is unimportant. The consequence is, as Schumacher noted: When our students do not come into contact with the self-shaping powers of large ideas, their lives are diminished. The future may hold great things, but the fact is, given the time-bound perspective out of which we always must know, the past holds even greater treasures. Our best ideas, values, and convictions have already been enacted and encoded in the classics. We persist in thinking that the best ideas lie in the future. That may be the case. But we have no way of knowing that. On the other hand, we can know with some clarity the ethical, legal, religious, scientific, philosophical, and political ideas that have already been thought. Whitehead once said that all of philosophy is a footnote to Plato, and he was very nearly right about that. No one in recent history has founded a world religion. Certainly our best political ideas come from classical sources. Henry Steele Commager once said that if we locked all the extant political scientists into the Kennedy School of Government for 30 years they would not produce what the Founding Fathers produced. We can learn as much from Augustine as Freud, more from Boethius than Wittgenstein, and in the passion of Abelard and Heloise glimpse a foreshadowing of the tangled paths of modern love.

So I am arguing that the materiality of the classics commands our attention. The voice of common sense says that a primary purpose of liberal education should be to impart the basic elements of that culture. Liberal education should convey a dramatic sense of what the greatest minds have thought, what the greatest artists have wrought, what the greatest leaders have done. The premier assumption of the liberal arts is that it is intrinsically worthwhile to know the great ideas and deeds that shaped the past and now shape us. This assumption does not deny the importance of new knowledge and recent discoveries. On the contrary. But once the Antaeus connection to the classical ground is broken, the liberal arts float aimlessly in a false element and are easily crushed. A liberally educated mind develops the ability to reach backwards in time, to identify imaginatively with the past. Without this vital connection, our mental and moral abilities are markedly foreshortened. John Henry Newman makes this point well in *The Idea of a University*. "The truly great intellect," he wrote, "is one which takes a connected view of the old and the new, past and present, far and near, and which has an insight into the influence of all these on one another without which there is no whole, no center."

It should be clear from what I have said that there can be no question of hypostasizing the classics. They are not the last word on the human adventure. They are only the last word to date. So they do not denote a static body of knowledge that is to be transmitted more or less mechanically. Kierkegaard has the apposite advice here, and his view nicely complements that of William James. Truth, Kierkegaard said, is something we appropriate, the manner in which we confront the great thought experiments of the past and the passion they arouse in us. Kierkegaard defined truth as "an appropriation process of the most passionate inwardness." Truth emerges when a funded body of knowledge is encountered by a free and inquiring mind. Kierkegaard himself labored mightily with traditional Christianity and the legacy of Hegel to produce his truth.

The second thread of my argument has to do with freedom. From this point of view, the classics can be seen as the record of the choices human beings have made. This point about freedom is analogous to my point about knowledge: Just as we cannot know anything new without knowing something old, so we cannot be free unless we study the record of human freedom. The classics are not only great thought experiments; they are also great enactments of freedom. In this sense, the classics are propaedeutic: They initiate us into the ways of freedom. G. K. Chesterton made this point in an interesting way. "We often talk about the past as though it were dead," he wrote, "but it is the future which is dead. The past moves on living lines, whereas the future is blind to the free part of human action." We know what people have chosen, we cannot know what they will choose.

The iconoclastic bias underlying our prevailing philosophies of education is future directed and tends to hold the past in low esteem. Modern intellectuals have a tendency to predicate the future on the demolition of the past. It is more or less assumed that the house of knowledge must be based on new foundations. "Make it new," Ezra Pound advised the poets, and educators have taken him more seriously than even the poets. On all sides, voices are raised to praise "plastic mobility," "open experience," "the apocalyptic imagination," and the "destructured self." Let us have done, they proclaim, with the old-centered notions of coherence and structure. The ethical imperative implicit in such pronouncements is that we must renounce belief in the possibility of gaining any reliable purchase on the continuity of human experience. (Deconstruction is the in-game in academia at the moment. And it is a lot of fun. The gist of the game is to take some classic text and "deconstruct" it by showing that it doesn't mean what we thought it meant, may mean the very opposite, or may mean nothing at all. But the irony of deconstruction is that it acknowledges a prior core, without which there would be nothing to deconstruct. Without the classics, the deconstructionists would be out of business tomorrow. As it turns out, they are the best read of our thinkers; they engage in a Kierkegaard-like struggle with masters like Plato, Descartes, Hegel, Nietzsche, and Heidegger. Although they often give the impression that the past is nugatory, in fact, it is a necessary condition of their whole enterprise. That is why I look upon deconstruction as a sincere freedom experiment.)

So our freedom is anchored in the past in the same way our knowledge is. Not more and not less. I am not thinking here of an abstract or merely private freedom, but of concrete political freedom as well. It is a good rule of thumb to assume a rather direct correspondence between the quality of education and the quality of political life. The concept of excellence that prevails in the one will prevail in the other. Conversely, to abandon the task of educating liberally is to abandon the principal means at our disposal for educating a responsible citizenry. This kind of education continues the tradition of civic humanism, which was worked out in the early Renaissance period, according to which the *studia humanitatis* (the study of the classics) formed the basis of political action. That tradition comes down through thinkers like Jefferson and Madison to John Dewey as a philosophy that combines critical intelligence with social action.

But we are having a hard time making that combination work today. Graduates of our best schools have performed ignominiously in the public arena. Students are largely apathetic toward the political process, toward civic values; woefully ignorant of the origin, history, and institutions of democratic values; indifferent to the multiple threats to freedom in our time—which in the end are threats to their own freedom. In this they do not differ greatly from the general populace. Americans in general have a weak sense of citizenship. As I read history, the last decade in which we as a nation showed a strong sense of citizenship was in the forties. We were at war then; we perceived it to be a good war; we were quite clear about what our ideals and values were; and we were drawn together in many creative ways to put our convictions into action.

That began to change in the fifties, primarily because the priorities of the nation became economic ones. We began to think of ourselves as consumers and professionals rather than as citizens. Education revamped to meet the demands of the market place, with the result that self-interest began disproportionately to displace the public interest. In the waning years of the century, our privatism has become virulent, rendering us insensitive to, and virtually powerless to deal effectively with, social pathologies of the most egregious kind. The dominant philosophy of our leaders has become what the social analyst Daniel Yankelovich calls "the money and missiles sense of reality." What really counts in this world "are military power and economic realities, and all the rest is sentimental stuff." On the other side of the fence, and speaking from the classical point of view, Mortimer Adler reminds us that the two most important things we have in common are the fact that we are all citizens and we are all philosophers, by which he means that we all have to think about what it means to be a citizen and to understand the basic ideas underlying citizenship. Since the first value of a democratic polity is freedom, I conclude this part of my argument with the thought that a primary task of liberal education is to lead students into a thorough investigation of freedom: its philosophy, its practices, its ethics, and its history.

And now for my final argument, which has to do with the story-telling function of the classics. It is helpful to think of education as a form of story telling. We are, as Robert Coles says, the story-telling creature because we ask questions about meaning. Story telling is the principal way in which we encounter reality: a way of asking questions about origins and destinies, of linking the private with the public, of arming ourselves against alienation, of sharing what we have learned with one another—in sum, the principal way in which we hold our sense of selfhood together. Because we are historical creatures, living our lives in the three dimensions of present, past, and future, everything we do necessarily becomes part of a story. Through fictions, metaphors, theories, and narratives, we make experience meaningful.

Hannah Arendt has developed a persuasive account of story telling based on the twin concepts of remembrance and reconciliation. The stories we read as children, so often beginning with "once upon a time," disclose the mystic pattern of human existence. They impart powerful messages about human achievement—about philosopher-kings, categorical imperatives, invisible hands, modes of production, gods and goddesses, quarks and quasars. Only great stories have the power to make us remember, and in remembering we forge an identity. Liberal education can erect a restraining wall against the contingency of the present and the lure of the future by driving deep into the mythic substance that forms the human pattern in any age. The connected mind is one that reaches deep into the collective memory of the race and measures its present possibilities for joy and despair, for victory and failure, against that memory. We all, says Arendt, "need to be reconciled to the world into which we were born strangers and in which we always remain strangers." Like the hero of Sartre's novel, *Nausea*, "we catch time by the tail" by turning our lives into a story. We overcome contingency, Sartre tell us, when the moments of our lives order themselves "like those of a life remembered." At this point, remembrance and reconciliation become part of a single act of self-affirmation.

I rest my case for the core on a metaphor: The classics are like the tain that reflect the images of human kind. The dictionary defines "tain" as a tinfoil suitable for backing mirrors. It is what enables us to see our reflection. Similarly, the classics form the backing of human